DECORATING WITH PICTURES

DECORATING WITH PICTURES

PICTURES

By Stephanie Hoppen

Major Photography by
Michael Hoppen and
Fritz von der Schulenburg

Clarkson Potter/Publishers
New York

All who would win joy, must share it;
happiness was born a twin.

LORD BYRON

TEXT BY CATHERINE HAIG

DESIGNED BY NANCY BUTKUS
AND LEIGH BRADFORD

Published by Clarkson N. Potter, Inc., 201 East 50th Street, New York, New York
10022. Member of the Crown Publishing Group.

CLARKSON POTTER, POTTER and colophon are trademarks of
Clarkson N. Potter, Inc.

Manufactured in Japan

Hoppen, Stephanie.
Decorating with pictures/by Stephanie Hoppen.
1. Pictures in interior decoration.   II. Title.
NK2115.5.P48H66   1991
747'.9—dc20   90-26932
ISBN 0-517-58168-X

1   3   5   7   9   10   8   6   4   2

First Edition

Contents

Introduction   ix

COLLECTING PICTURES

$\mathcal{I}$NTRODUCTION

I love collecting pictures. My whole way of thinking about life, my whole viewpoint, is affected by the things I have around me. I was lucky to grow up among beautiful objects and to have a mother who had a great sense of her own style. Our house contained an extraordinary mixture of the old and the new, reflecting her passion for lovely things and lack of adherence to any strict rules. Her table was always decorated with flowers and fruit, and she served coffee after dinner in a set of Harlequin coffee cups and saucers—each different and each beautiful. My memory of our house is a wonderful kaleidoscope of colors and textures. My school friends, too, remember it as different from any other, and my mother's garden was so special that people came from all over the world to walk through it and marvel at its beauty. She used to take me with her when she visited our local antiques shops and auctions, and so, as I grew up, I absorbed an awareness of beautiful furnishings and objects, and particularly pictures.

Pictures, I firmly believe, are the soul of a house. China, glass, fabrics, rugs, furniture are all fascinating and essential elements of the home and are rewarding in their own right, but pictures are different. Pictures say a great deal about the character of the owner, and a collection of pictures brings an extraordinary sense of originality and uniqueness to a house. But many homes, particularly American ones, are notable for their lack of pictures. People tend to be nervous about making a statement with pictures and it is the aim of this book to help them break through their fear and reticence.

If you have spent time in museums and galleries and have been exposed to art, you have probably already developed a discriminating eye. Forget about good taste or bad taste, doing the right thing or the wrong thing. Instead, just do what you like because you really like it, not because you feel you should.

If you feel uncertain about what is good and what you like, there are ways in which to help yourself gain the confidence to evolve your own style. Start by looking around you. Study the picture collections in your local museums and become a regular visitor to your local art galleries, antiques shops, and auction houses. Viewing the big

sales is an addictive pastime and a fascinating way to learn about the great masters, while at the bottom of a pile of tattered prints in a smaller sale you might come across an unexpected treasure. Not only will you gain knowledge about artists and craftsmen, both old and new, but you will gain an important feel for the market. Auction rooms and shops offer an indication of current trends, and art school shows point to future ones: Watch what people buy and for how much and try to work out why. Choose a gallery, antiques shop, or art dealer whose taste you admire and make a point of asking why this picture is so much more or less than

that one. Study, too, the numerous "bibles" of interior design that flood the newsstands each month. Photographs of the homes of top decorators, collectors, and others with style will provide you with expert advice. What sort of pictures do they collect? How do they frame them? How do they group and hang them? This "foundation course" in art, both past and present, will gradually give you the confidence to begin building up your own collection, based on your own personal taste rather than what is considered to

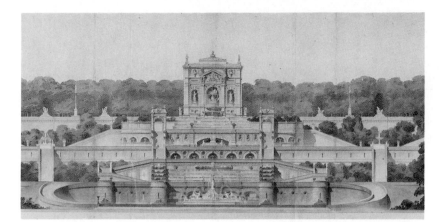

be "right" or "wrong." Buying pictures can be enormous fun and whether you buy through a dealer or bid for a knock-down "masterpiece" at auction or spend a Saturday morning browsing at a flea market or antiques show, the joy of collecting remains the same.

Pictures are infinitely diverse—there is always, happily, something for everybody. It does not matter whether you line your walls with rare old masters, prints from a local antiques shop, black-and-white photographs, or your children's doodles, just as long as they appeal to you. They will probably outlast any other element in your decorative scheme, so the fact that you like your pictures is of primary importance.

A collection need—indeed, should—never be static. As a glance at this book will show, the concept of one lonely picture hanging in isolated grandeur is not one I favor. I love lots of pictures. I love mixing differ-

ent media and different subject matter. I love framing some identically, some differently, and I love the effect that simply regrouping or reframing a collection of pictures can have on a room. A collection of pictures takes time to amass, time to evolve, and is ever-changing as new pictures come and old ones are reframed and re-hung. It is a living, growing thing:

but don't be frightened by it. Use it, tame it, tailor it to your own likes and needs.

I believe that now, more than ever before, people are cherishing their homes as places of sanctuary from the world outside. Life in the 1990s is fast-moving, hard-talking, and aggressive, and we need to be able to retreat to somewhere very special, very warm, and very cozy—a place filled with things that we love, things that give us pleasure and enhance our daily lives.

COLLECTING PICTURES

In the following pages I show examples of pictures that can afford great pleasure, some of them chosen because they are particularly important, some because they will be the themes of the future, and some simply because they are my favorites. There are numerous other genres. To list but a few: photography; caricature, from Hogarth and Gilray right up to the great cartoonists of today; the American illustrators of the nineteenth century such as Currier & Ives; paintings of the naive school; the ancient art forms of silhouettes, trompe l'oeil, and decoupage (a form of cut-out collage, very popular in the nineteenth century); needlework and embroidery, including, of course, those beautiful samplers worked in such painstaking detail by little girls through the centuries. Pictures for your collection need never be restricted by the aesthetic dictates of others. The only criterion must be that you collect what appeals to you.

NIMALS IN ART

Animals are a perennial favorite with artists and collectors alike. In the hang-dog expression of a faithful hound or the self-satisified smirk of a prize hog, there is something delightfully cozy and comforting, offering a homely contrast to high-tech life.

Animal pictures can be found rendered in watercolor or oil or as prints in an enormous variety of styles. These range from the most primitive depictions of prize domestic farm animals to the most sophisticated portraits of sleek thoroughbred racehorses. Generally speaking, in the field of naive art, animals tended to be more favored by British artists than by their American counterparts, and, in particular, dogs, since every English country gentleman made sure there was at least one por-

trait of the family hound. The squire might have had his gun dog or horse painted; the yeoman farmer, his prize pig, bull, or sheep.

Again, there are many ways to collect: Some people prefer to concentrate on one particular kind of animal, creating a wall of, say, dogs or pigs or horses or that perennially chic subject,

Two works by contemporary English artists who paint in the style of the past: LEFT, a head of a dog in oil by Mid; RIGHT, a portrait in oil of a trio of dachshunds by Dan Dunton.

Lady Mary, Nip & Buff

...operty of Lady Jane Murray of Banner Cross in the County of *Yorkshire*.   D.D

the monkey, so often portrayed in gentlemen's clothes. Others prefer to mix the species but concentrate on a particular style.

Although demand for eighteenth- and nineteenth-century naive animal paintings has pushed prices way beyond the reach of the average collector, happily there are still artists in America and England painting today in this primitive style. And, of course, prints are easily found in antiques shops. These pictures, whether grouped en masse or used singly or in pairs, lend a room every bit as much character as their earlier counterparts.

ABOVE and RIGHT: Two oils by contemporary English artist Paul Stagg, who paints in the primitive style.

LEFT: A collection of animal paintings combines happily with animal ornaments in one corner of this sitting room. ABOVE and BELOW: Two works in the primitive English style by Dan Dunton.

Nollekens
The faithful friend of Master Edward & Miss Mary Cox Macro of Little Haugh Hall

A collection of eight
dog paintings by English
contemporary artists.

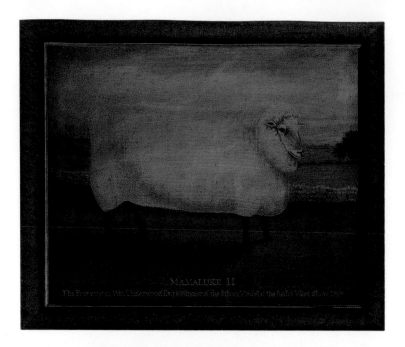

MAMALUKE II
The Property of Will Underwood Esq & Winner of the Silver Medal at the Bath & West Show 1849

Lord Adolphus
The Prize Short horn Bull, the Property of Jonas Webb Esq. of Pilton House in the County of Norfolk

Two typical English country pictures, both 20th century: ABOVE LEFT, stylized sheep; LEFT, a prize bull. ABOVE RIGHT: A more formal portrait of a whippet. OPPOSITE: A whimsical dog portrait by Mid.

BALLOONS

A wonderfully whimsical area for collecting is the depiction of balloons or *Montgolfiers* as they are known in France after their inventors, the brothers Joseph and Jacques Etienne Montgolfier. This duo lived in the latter half of the eighteenth century, and, fascinated by earlier aeronautical theories, they constructed a balloon that was lifted by lighting a cauldron of paper beneath it. They achieved a flight of six miles, but further experiments were frustrated by the outbreak of the French Revolution.

It is not difficult to understand the attraction of balloon pictures. They are not only charming, decorative, and scientifically interesting, they also symbolize escape to a fantasy, fairy-tale world. They are, however, becoming increasingly rare, and even late-nineteenth- and early-twentieth-century examples are hard to find. A group of the illustrations we show here are by a contemporary French artist, Marie Amalia, who not only captures the whimsical charm of this wonderful subject but also employs the unusual and ancient technique of reverse painting on glass. The results are charming.

Enlèvement de la Machine Aérostatique au Jardin des Thuileries en 1783.

A collection of late-19th-century and early-20th-century French prints of balloons. LEFT: A heliogravure entitled "Balloon taking off, Paris."

A quintet of balloon paintings, executed in reverse on glass by the contemporary French artist Marie Amalia.

ARCHITECTURE AS DECORATION

The decorative value of architectural watercolors, drawings, and engravings has long been appreciated by top decorators on both sides of the Atlantic. Not only is this an incredibly detailed and sophisticated form of art, it also recalls the golden ages of building through the centuries, bringing the timeless elegance of eras past into our homes today. This is, however, a look that takes a great deal of care and attention to achieve; grouping, mounting, framing, and hanging are crucial.

Architecture as a subject is strong, decisive, and uncompromising. The clean lines and often monochromatic tones of architectural prints and drawings lend themselves particularly well to use in offices, halls, studies, dressing rooms, and other more masculine settings. They do not blend easily with other subject matter, but look best in a group, hung with strict regard for symmetry and order.

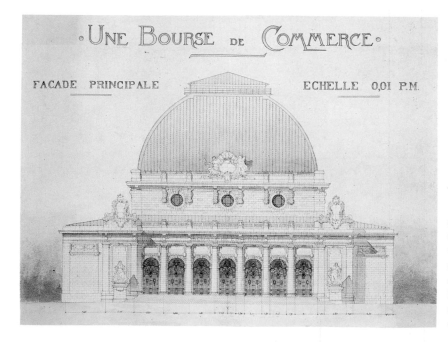

Three fine examples of 19th-century Beaux Arts architectural drawing, all executed in pencil and color wash. LEFT: Proposed design for a French Bourse de Commerce. ABOVE: Detail of an architectural order. RIGHT: Study of a classical capital.

TEMPLE
DE
JUPITER·STATOR

DETAIL·AU·QUART·DE·L'EXECUTION

ABOVE: A mid-19th-century
Beaux Arts study of an
elevation, executed in pencil
and watercolor. RIGHT: An
unusually large watercolor
of a church in the Middle
East, perhaps in Lebanon,
dating from the 1800s.

PALACIO A.HEBER JACKSON

Two watercolor works by the contemporary Hungarian artist Andras Kaldor, depicting the opera house in Berlin, TOP, and the Athenaeum in London, ABOVE. RIGHT: French 19th-century study for an ornately carved and detailed column, topped by Napoleon, and resembling the one in the Place Vendôme in Paris.

LEFT: A 19th-century design for a very grand town house, probably in Buenos Aires.

ABOVE: A 19th-century design for the façade of a railway station in the south of France. FAR LEFT: Watercolor of the Zurich opera house by Andras Kaldor. LEFT: Watercolor of a typical French 19th-century Château, designed in brick and stone, with a high-hipped roof and graceful curving outer staircase. RIGHT: A collection of architectural renderings, hung and stacked frame-touching-frame, to create a dramatic point of interest in this sitting room.

FLOWERS ARE ETERNAL

Flowers in art have undergone such a dramatic revival during the past ten years—along with flowers in chintz, wallpaper, and china—that it is easy to forget they have been a perennial subject for artists. There is barely a painter, past or present, who has not rendered flowers in some form or other, and as long as people love gardens, flower prints and paintings will always be popular.

More than any other subject matter, flowers serve to bring the peace and tranquility of the country into the home. They bring softness and color to even the innermost city apartment and look well in almost any scheme. A favorite bedroom accessory, they can also enrich a drawing room, dining room, kitchen, or study, enhancing a traditional chintzy scheme or softening a more modern, monochromatic effect. Indeed, it is hard to imagine a room without flowers of some kind!

Few of us can afford the wonderful floral still lifes which were available a hundred or even fifty years ago. But it is still possible to find botanical prints by the great names of the seventeenth, eighteenth, and nineteenth centuries;

ABOVE: A royal monogram in flowers by Tessier, the famous 18th-century flower painter. RIGHT: An evocative 19th-century English watercolor.

artists of great talent such as Maria Sybilla Merian, who traveled to South America in 1698 to record the insects and flowers of that region. Basil Besler, Georg Dionysius Ehret, Pierre Joseph Redoute, Jean Louis Prevost, Franz and Ferdinand Bauer, Walter Hood Fitch, and James Sowerby are just a few other notable names; the list is long, the output prolific. Alternatively, look out for contemporary painters of flowers; the work of Spanish artist José Escofet, my favorite, is now well known, but there are always new and talented artists coming up to watch for.

Everyone has his or her own method of collecting. A pretty way of featuring botanical illustrations or watercolors is to concentrate on one particular flower. A wall full of auriculas or tulips or roses can look wonderful, and the sum of all the pictures together is very much more dramatic than showing each one singly. I personally like to mix engravings, watercolors, and oils, for an enchanting "nosegay" effect.

Painting on a dark background was a popular conceit in the late 18th and 19th centuries. Here are 18th-, 19th-, and 20th-century variations on this theme. ABOVE: Irises in a blue-and-white jar by José Escofet.

ABOVE: An early-19th-century English gouache. LEFT: A basket of anemones by José Escofet. RIGHT: Two floral studies by the 18th-century German artist Barbara Regina Dietzsch.

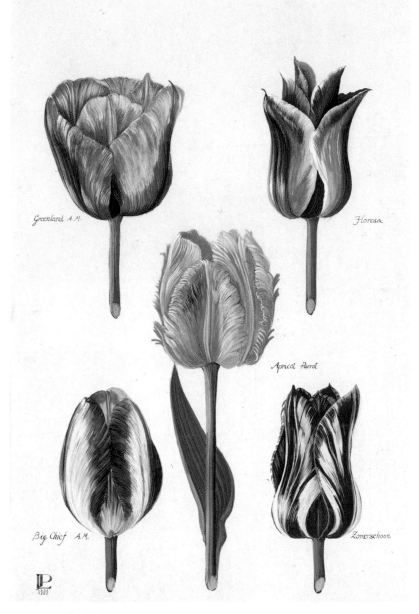

ABOVE: Geraniums, gouache by José Escofet.
BELOW: A floral plate from Maria Sybilla Merian's *History of the Insects of Europe*, 1683.

A quintet of tulip heads painted in gouache on vellum by contemporary artist Luca Palermo.

ABOVE: Daffodils in a vase, gouache, by José Escofet. BELOW: Hand-colored botanical engraving of poppies by Crispin de Passe, 1617.

A tulip in watercolor from a 17th-century Dutch grower's catalogue of tulip varieties, flanked by vases of real tulips.

The auricula is a flower with an almost-cult following, portrayed by artists through the ages. Here we show a selection in watercolor and gouache.

LEFT and RIGHT: Four studies by José Escofet. TOP and ABOVE: A pair by an unknown 19th-century artist.

A wall of auriculas, hung closely for maximum
effect. Studies by José Escofet, TOP, and Luca
Palermo, ABOVE.

A 19th-century watercolor of a room in an Austrian palace, showing its wonderfully intricate sugar-icing plasterwork.

THE LURE OF INTERIORS

A rich, rather somber 19th-century French interior painted in oil.

House interiors have always exercised an extraordinary fascination. From the early Dutch still lifes of Vermeer to watercolors of seventeenth-century Swedish palaces to Vuillard's intimate oil paintings, this subject matter has long satisfied a vital need. Before the advent of the camera, the artist's brush was the only way in which succeeding generations of proud home owners could record the decorative delights of their own houses. And, thanks to these artists, we now have a legacy of highly detailed and intimate glimpses into the past, painted both by professionals and amateurs, some known, many anonymous, and commissioned by a whole spectrum of society from princes down to the bourgeoisie.

This treasure trove is augmented by designs from the fashionable curtainmakers, upholsterers, and interior decorators of the eighteenth and nineteenth centuries, who painted examples of their handicraft with detail and exactitude for their important or potential clients to view. Some of these designs come down to us in their original watercolor form; others were reproduced as prints.

This genre has reached new heights of popularity today, increasing in value and price. In watercolor, oil, and print, it exercises a continuing fascination in much the same way as do interior decorating magazines and books: offering a fleeting yet highly intimate glimpse of how others live, interesting enough when the setting is contemporary and particularly riveting when it tells of times and conventions past.

Paintings of interiors can be used to marvelous effect. To my mind, this genre looks best not en masse but in groups of three or four, to create a wonderfully intimate corner. Happily, despite the photographer's skills, this is an art revived.

A pastel of an interior with a Scandinavian feel. Note the painted screen and the pair of fire screens in front of the mantelpiece.

Four interiors executed in typically 19th-century manner, with perspective sacrificed to the desire to portray every element in the room. TOP AND TOP RIGHT: Prints from a rare book on German Biedermeier.

LEFT: A French watercolor. ABOVE: A watercolor of English provenance. RIGHT: A group of 19th-century interiors combine with a mirror and a decorative wall sconce to create an intimate corner in a very grand room.

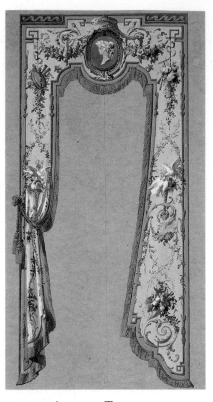

ABOVE and BELOW: Two watercolor renderings of curtains by 19th-century French curtain-makers.

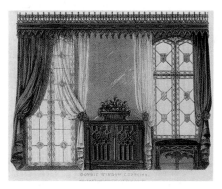

A 19th-century chromolithograph of a luxuriant French bedroom, complete with tented ceiling and half-tester bed.

TOP LEFT and TOP RIGHT:
Two watercolor designs by
Fiona Saunders for a 19th-
century French bed by
David Mlinaric and Tom
Parr respectively.

The other watercolor
renderings are by 19th-
century French curtain-
makers, one (BELOW
CENTER) topped with
an ornamental gilt
pelmet board.

The Little Fountain. Drakelowe —
Beatrice Parsons

A charming watercolor by Beatrice Parsons (1870–1955) of Drakelowe in Derbyshire, a typically English Edwardian country garden, its herbaceous borders in full bloom.

Gardens

Gardens have always been a favorite subject for both the amateur and the professional artist and highly prized by collectors, too. The earliest drawings and engravings of garden designs are now of enormous historical importance, particularly when they illustrate the great eighteenth-century gardens of Europe. When the gardens and parks are like those laid out by masters such as "Capability" Brown and Humphry Repton that still exist, the drawings have added relevance.

These, however, are museum pieces —beyond the reach of the average collector—and though they are fascinating to study, we have to find alternatives. Sketching and painting were approved accomplishments for every Victorian lady, and many a Victorian border was captured for posterity as a result, but these, too, are much sought-after today. Along with the current mania for everything Victorian, the prices of nineteenth-century garden paintings have soared.

Much more reasonable are eighteenth- and nineteenth-century prints of gardens and garden designs, which, with clever framing, can look very pretty grouped on a wall. Or look at the work of living artists such as Pedro Darder in Spain, who has painted many scenes from his own beautiful garden, or John Warrender in England, who paints bird's-eye views of contemporary gardens in the seventeenth-century manner.

A grandly ornamented
conservatory in
Lincolnshire, painted in
watercolor by contemporary
artist Sally Maltby.

ABOVE LEFT: Ryan's Path, a watercolor by Rosemary Clark Stiefel of Ryan Gainey's garden, near her home in Atlanta. LEFT: A watercolor sketch for a proposed ornamental well in a French garden, dating from the early 20th century. ABOVE: A watercolor by Sally Maltby of the spiral staircase at Kew.

ABOVE: A 19th-century
watercolor of an English
garden, with topiary and
herbaceous borders by
E. A. Rolfe of Suffolk.
RIGHT: Watercolor of a
classical temple in an Italian
garden, dating from the
19th century.

ABOVE: A very large
watercolor depicting the
refurbishment of the
fountains at Clichy by
architects Lefuel and
Coquart, dating from the
19th century. RIGHT: A
formal parterre interspersed
with statuary in this 19th-
century Italian oil painting.

ABOVE: A typical early-18th-century Temple of Love in a French garden in watercolor. RIGHT: Two hand-colored engravings of gardens by an unknown German engraver, c. 1700.

A French watercolor of the
park at Versailles, dating
from the 19th century.

A trio of late-19th-century and early-20th-century fashion drawings. LEFT: "Laissez-moi-seule," a plate for *Les Feuillets d'Art,* 1919, by George Barbier, the great fashion designer and illustrator and one of the leading figures of the Art Deco movement. FAR RIGHT: Two original watercolors for advertisements by the Danish painter, fashion designer, and illustrator Gerda Wegener, dated Copenhagen 1889–1914.

ASHION

Fashion prints have always been a prime collecting area. In the nineteenth century, "magazines" of fashion plates were the only way to keep abreast of the new fashions emerging in the capital or at court, and these illustrations are now much sought after as pretty bedroom, bathroom, or dressing-room accessories. The covers of fashion magazines in our own century, such as Erte's celebrated drawings for *Vogue*, are also perennially popular.

A rather more unusual aspect of fashion collecting, however, recently came to my attention when I bought a collection of about eighty watercolors of shoes and boots. They were extraordinarily popular partly for reasons of demand—pictures of shoes are quite rare—and partly because shoes have always held a strange and inexplicable lure for women (witness the Victoria and Albert Museum's 1987 exhibition of Ferragamo shoes).

Though shoe pictures are rare, these examples illustrate how attractive and amusing it can be to concentrate a collection around one article of clothing. It would be just as effective to look for pictures of hats, hat pins, or belts.

Early-20th-century
chromolithograph.

ABOVE **and** FAR RIGHT:
Three examples from a rare
collection of late-19th-
and early-20th-century
watercolors of shoes.

ABOVE and ABOVE LEFT: Two prints typical of the genre that appeared in the *Gazette du Bon Ton,* a famous fashion magazine founded in 1912, which featured the top couturiers and best illustrators of the day.

Four more striking examples from the
collection of watercolor shoe pictures.

ABOVE: **Sampling the cuisine**, by Jean Beraud. OPPOSITE: **The Parisian flower shop** by Victor Gilbert.

LOVELY LADIES

Heliogravure was a form of printing developed in the last quarter of the nineteenth century that made prints appear like watercolors. The technique was experimental—like so much that was going on in the world of industry and science at that time—and proved phenomenally expensive, ultimately pricing itself out of existence. Practitioners reproduced the work of such well-known nineteenth-century Parisian artists as Paul César, Helleu, Emile Buyard, Victor Gilbert, Jean Beraud, L. Doucet, Pierre Carrier Belleuse, and Tofano. They—and others—have left behind a legacy of these prints-cum-watercolors, most of which depict romantic and theatrical Parisian scenes: elegantly dressed ladies going to the races, walking by the sea, buying flowers, and so on. Heliogravures are difficult to find, but once found they are not prohibitively expensive.

ABOVE: Oriental-looking
"Balerine," after L. Leloir.
ABOVE RIGHT: At the
theater, heliogravure by
H. Kaemmerer. BELOW
RIGHT: A dancer by Pierre
Carrier Belleuse.

A lady at her dressing
table by L. Doucet.

ABOVE: **Shrimp fishing by L. Doucet.** RIGHT: **Lady on a bridge by F. Heilbuth.**

LEFT: A skating party by
L. Doucet. ABOVE: Lady in
a muff by the English artist
C. H. Boughton.

$\mathcal{S}$TILL LIFE

TOP: **A delightfully intimate French 19th-century still life by J. Rec.** ABOVE: **Blue-and-white faience by contemporary Spanish artist Manuel Blesa.**

Still life is one of the most timeless and universally adored forms of art. A simple composition of everyday objects such as flowers and fruit, a jug, a vase, or a ceramic bowl seems to appeal to every generation. Still lives of objects that appear in almost every home are easy to relate to, and in much the same way as pictures of interiors, they provide a tantalizing glimpse of life in that particular household at that particular moment. Times change and fashions change but still life—or *nature mort* as the French call it—survives.

A decade or so ago, it was still possible to buy a fine still life in oil, dating from the nineteenth, eighteenth, or even seventeenth century, for a reasonable sum. Today, these pictures are prohibitively expensive. Nineteenth-century prints and watercolors are an attractive alternative: These convey all the charm of the still life composition at affordable prices. Once again, do not neglect artists painting today: This is a timeless genre still much practiced today in England, America, and also throughout Europe.

A collection of red
and white currants
and peaches resting
on a stone ledge by
Michel Bouillon,
circa 1610—1660,
oil on copper.

A 19th-century Spanish still
life in oil.

A trio of evocative still lifes
by José Escofet.

Gateau de Noel, executed in reverse on glass by Marie Amalia.

$\mathcal{G}$OURMANDISES

In both America and England over the past few years there has been an enormous rise of interest in food. You have only to look at the number of specialty food shops that have sprouted along every sidewalk, and the explosion of books dealing with food and entertaining, to note this trend. And there has also been a corresponding interest in pictures that, quite unashamedly, depict food in all guises.

Obviously most suitable to hang in a dining room or kitchen, these pictures can take the form of still life arrangements of food on a table or sideboard; they can be highly detailed, botanical studies of fruit and vegetables; and they can be amusing and lighthearted, such as Christine Thouzeau's delightful cake. Even a decorative menu, framed in a simple lacquer frame, can be fun

to hang on a wall, particularly if it serves as a reminder of a special celebration or meal.

This seems to me to be an area that will become increasingly popular in the near future; meanwhile, look out for food pictures—they are fun to collect, fun to look at, and there are still bargains to be had.

LEFT: **Bowl of asparagus, watercolor on silk by Patzi Craven.** ABOVE: **Strawberry pyramid cake, watercolor by Christine Thouzeau.**

An "advertisement" for seeds by the famous French company Vilmorin, dating from the 19th century.

ABOVE: A late-19th-century watercolor of a greengrocer with his wares by an unknown artist. RIGHT: Watercolor of a cabbage by Miriam Escofet.

A pair of delightful watercolors by Christine Thouzeau, a contemporary French artist and illustrator, showing sheets of music wrapped around flowers and *pommes frites.*

RIGHT: A 19th-century portrait in oil of a French bourgeois couple. BELOW: A page of early-18th-century hand-colored engravings of English coats-of-arms.

$\mathcal{I}$NSTANT ANCESTORS

One of the most exciting features of any European ancestral home was always the picture gallery, a long room lined, often from floor to ceiling, with paintings. Sometimes these comprised a haphazard collection gathered on the Grand Tour by several generations of the same family; while some of the most wonderful of these rooms were portrait galleries in which many generations of the family were depicted, often by the great painters of their day.

Few of us have picture galleries, much less access to such paintings from our ancestors, but the "picture gallery look" is a fascinating concept, particularly when dealing with a specific area of a house such as an awkwardly shaped room or passage. Please note, however, that this is a look that cannot be created overnight. It is an effect that is best built up over years. But don't despair: with careful hanging, it can look just as good while it is growing.

Portrait of a Spanish grandee wearing the Order of Alcantara and Santiago, with his wife and three children, dated 1634, by Wolfgang Heimbach. The Castle of Santelmo is in the distance.

LEFT: Watercolor of a young English girl by an unknown artist, circa 1820.
OPPOSITE: Michael Szell created a dramatic effect by placing grand portraits and other paintings against a background of bold color and large-scale design.

Portrait by Antonio Carnicero of the Marques de Penafiel, elder son of the Duke of Osuna, dated 1811.

RIGHT: French portrait in pastel, typical of the genre frequently commissioned by the bourgeoisie in the late 18th and early 19th centuries.

Portraits line the walls of this elegant stairway in Luttrellstown House, a historic country house in Ireland.

LEFT: An 18th-century portrait of an unknown French provincial lady.

BELOW LEFT: A particularly fine 19th-century print of a central European lady.

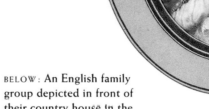

BELOW: An English family group depicted in front of their country house in the style of the 19th century.

ABOVE: A French 18th-century portrait, possibly of Madame de Sevigny,

ANTHROPOMORPHIC PORTRAITS

Anthropomorphic portraiture—that is, the combination of animals' heads superimposed upon human bodies, or the reverse—is a genre that appears and reappears throughout the history of painting. The satyr of classical mythology, a man's head upon a horse's body, and the devil were frequently portrayed as part human, part animal. In the seventeenth and eighteenth centuries, monkeys were often the focus of this quirky and essentially tongue-in-cheek form of art, and, later, the development of political caricature offered another outlet, with public figures ridiculed in appropriate—and always recognizable—animal form.

A contemporary artist has taken this genre of portraiture a lighthearted step farther. Thierry Poncelet, a picturer restorer, searches out old portraits in poor condition and paints an appropriate animal's head—usually a dog, cat, or monkey—onto the original sitter. He then restores the rest of the canvas, creating a delightfully humorous new-from-old work of art.

THIS PAGE and OVERLEAF: A selection of the quirky and amusing portraits created by Thierry Ponçelet, who replaces the original sitter's face with an animal's head.

ABOVE: Oil on copper of an early tennis match, painted in 19th-century style by an unknown artist. ABOVE RIGHT: An original watercolor of a "sporting" couple, from the 1920s.

$\mathcal{S}$PORT

This is a thoroughly traditional area, covering the classic country pursuits of hunting, shooting, fishing, and racing, as well as games such as cricket, tennis, golf, and croquet. Sporting pictures tend to divide into two categories: first, the works by the great sporting artists such as Stubbs and Sartorius, which are masterpieces commanding masterpiece prices, and so not really within the scope of this book; and second, the pictures that relate to one's own particular sporting hobby—prints of cricket or racing or golf, for example —which make an amusing theme for a collection, perhaps combined with old team photographs. . . .

Sport was traditionally an English country gentleman's pastime, and every English country house would have its complement of sporting pictures. The great age of the sporting print was the first half of the nineteenth century and featured famous names such as Thomas

Rowlandson, George Morland, J. F. Herring, James Pollard, and F. C. Turner. These are still immensely popular today—though expensive—and many galleries specialize in this genre.

There is often an element of humor in sporting pictures, and this, together with their appeal to modern-day sportsmen, makes them enjoyable to collect. A fanatical golfer might like golfing pictures to line the walls of his —or her—study; a racehorse owner might prefer paintings of past legends of the turf or even to commission paintings of his own winners. There is generally something for everyone.

ABOVE: Chromolithograph of a fish from a book entitled *Game Fishes of the United States* by S. A. Kilbourne, 1879. ABOVE RIGHT: Late-19th-century French watercolor of harness racing. RIGHT: A print of several yachts participating in the America's Cup, dating from the 19th century.

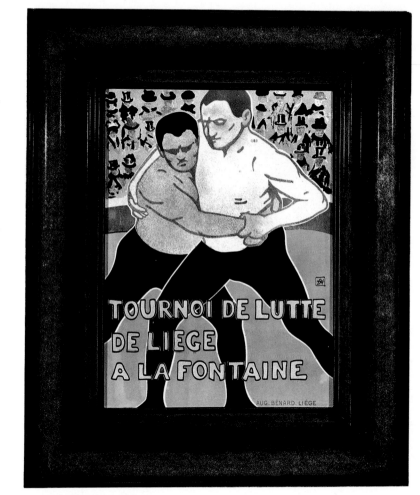

ABOVE: *Tournoi de lutte*, lithograph dated 1899, advertising a wrestling match. ABOVE RIGHT: A 19th-century English watercolor of a hunting scene. RIGHT: A very early 20th-century print in full color of a golf match sponsored by a whiskey company.

ABOVE: A rare French print of a rugby match, dating from the late 19th century. ABOVE RIGHT: A late-19th-century hand-colored print of a racehorse. RIGHT: A very early hand-colored engraving of a cricket match, dating from about 1800.

A cricket print by Cecil Alden, dated 1905, one of a set of twelve depicting old British sports.

ABOVE: Derby Day at
Flemington Racecourse,
Melbourne, is captured in
this 19th-century hand-
colored print. RIGHT: Oil
on copper of a polo match,
date and artist unknown.

SHELLS AND SEA CREATURES

In the seventeenth and eighteenth centuries, shells were much prized by collectors, who paid huge sums for these beautiful novelties, brought home by explorers from around the world. These collections were recorded in shell books such as Thomas Martyn's *The Universal Conchologist*, published 1784 to 1787. For the purpose of his books, Martyn bought a collection of shells brought back by Captain Cook from a voyage to the South Seas, and employed a studio of young artists to provide the illustrations for the 160 hand-colored plates. Today, shell prints such as these are very rare and highly sought after, but it is still possible to find attractive later prints at more reasonable prices.

Pictures of shells, fish, and other sea creatures make popular subjects for beach houses, and they also work well in bathrooms and kitchens. Cleverly framed—perhaps as a series—they can look marvelous grouped on one wall in, say, an entrance hall or on a stairway. They are fun to collect and, individually, make an interesting alternative to the more usual subjects such as flowers, animals, or fruit.

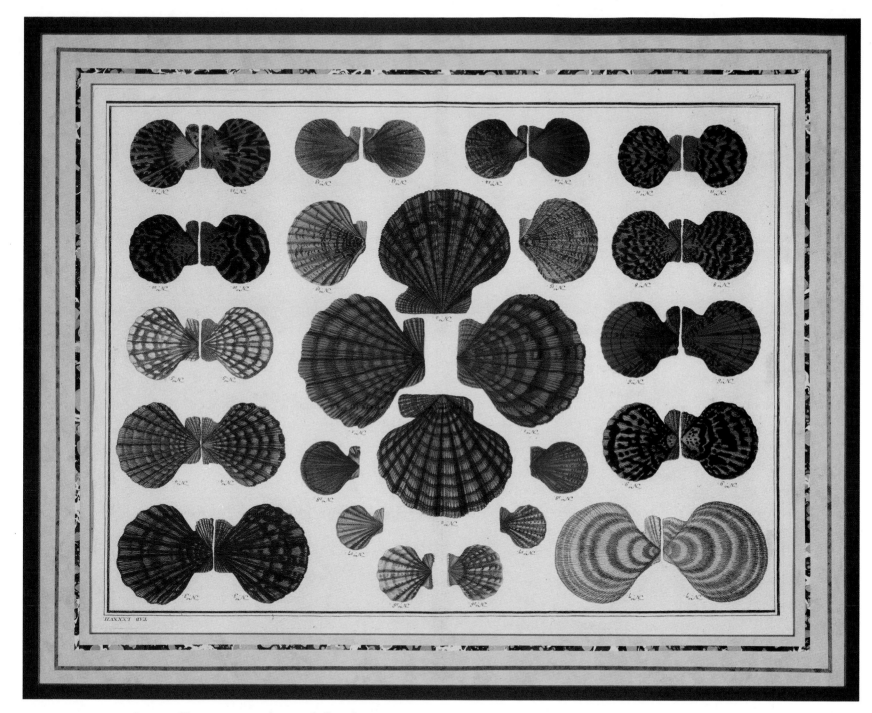

OPPOSITE BOTTOM and ABOVE: Two engravings of exotic shells and crustacea
from Albertus Seba's *Cabinet of Curiosities,* 1734–1765. A German
apothecary, Seba was the greatest collector of natural curiosities the world has
ever known. He collated and drew everything he owned in order to produce
this fine four-volume work.

Five more detailed
engravings of shells and
crustacea from Seba's
Cabinet of Curiosities.

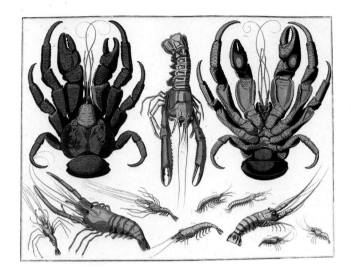

A French 19th-century
chromolithograph of a
catch of fish.

DUCKS AND BIRDS

Almost every species of birds has been recorded at some point by artists around the world. The great age of bird books with their beautiful, hand-colored plates, was the nineteenth century and includes the great artists and ornithologists such as Audubon, Gould, and Lear. John James Audubon was fascinated by birds from early childhood and gradually evolved his "great idea," to record, life size, every species of bird in America. His book, *The Birds of America*, published between 1827 and 1838, contained no fewer than 435 hand-colored aquatint plates.

Birds still seem to exercise a great fascination, from the startled grouse or partridge of the sporting print to the flamboyant plumage of the exotic ornithological specimen. Indeed, there is a contemporary Audubon working today in Zimbabwe; his name is Robert Finch, and despite rapidly failing eyesight, he has dedicated himself to recording all the species of Southern Africa. His work is in the great tradition of bird artists.

Bird prints and paintings are relatively easy to find—although prices vary enormously. A collection of duck pictures grouped with a pair of painted wood decoy ducks illustrates what can be done by concentrating on one particular species. Alternatively, a disparate collection of birds, all framed differently, can look marvelous in a study or hallway or hung in progression up a stairway.

OPPOSITE: Watercolor of a barn owl by Robert Finch. ABOVE: An example from Audubon's monumental work, *The Birds of America*, 1827–1838.

A 19th-century drawing of two classical heads.

Collection of framed intaglio seals and wax impressions, dating from the 18th and 19th centuries.

LIFE STUDIES

The quiet, cool elegance of the neoclassical seems to me to be the latest trend in interior design, perhaps simply a reaction of the past decade, with its emphasis on chintz, color, and pattern. Whatever the reasons, there has been a parallel revival of interest in neoclassical art and objets d'art.

One aspect of this genre that is still relatively under-appreciated—and therefore of particular interest to the new collector—is life studies. Primarily executed in charcoal, sepia, sanguine, or pencil, these drawings were, and are, mostly the work of art students, sketching from life or from classical sculpture. Indeed, art schools around the world must be full of such studies, submitted by generations of students—if one could but have access to them. One does stumble across life studies in the most unlikely junk shops and flea markets, and it is still possible to find a fine late-nineteenth-century studio drawing for under a thousand dollars.

This is a field in which the interplay of pictures and objects is very effective. Framed collections of intaglio seals, statues, busts, and architectural objects would all serve to put a group of life studies into context. And even these do not have to be priceless antiquities: several museums, such as the Victoria and Albert in London, are producing replicas of some of the statues and busts in their collections.

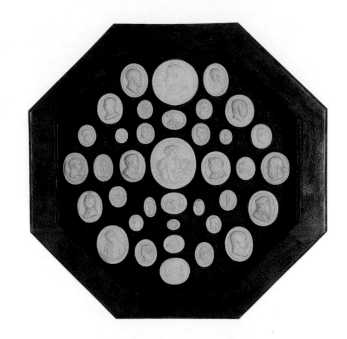

LEFT: A marvelous grouping of neo-classical objects and drawings, including 18th-century plaster-ware and a fine bust. RIGHT: A group of white plaster intaglio seals in a beautiful octagonal frame. BELOW: Red wax intaglio seals in a gold-leaf frame.

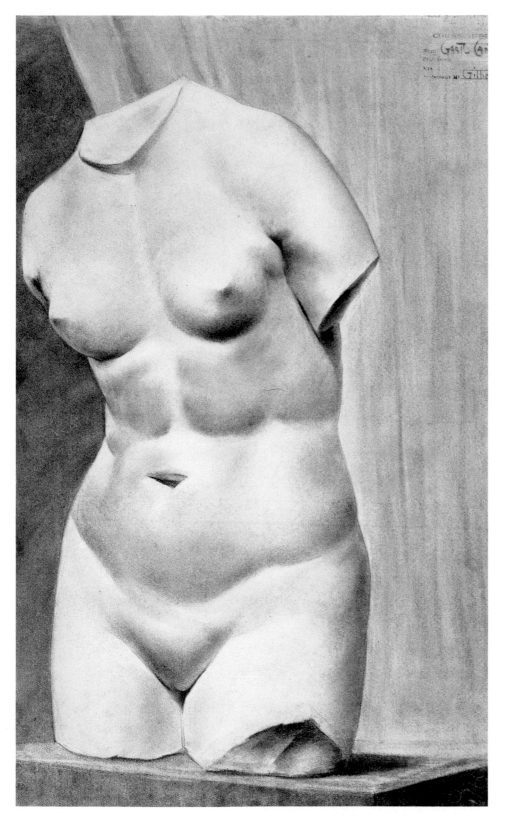

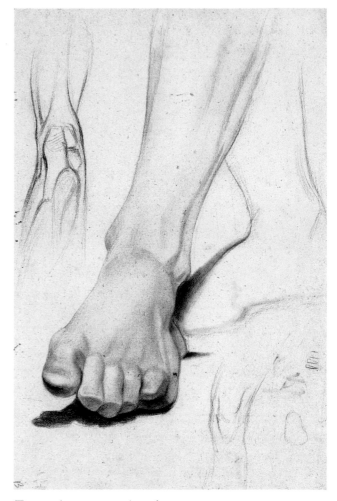

Two 19th-century studies of
a female torso and foot.

LEFT: A detail of the desk in couturier Karl Lagerfeld's home, featuring an elegant selection of neoclassical objects. ABOVE: A 19th-century drawing of a head. ABOVE RIGHT: An 18th-century drawing of a classical figure. RIGHT: Late-19th-century or early-20th-century French oil painting of an artist painting a nude model, a typical life study but unusual in that it is in oil rather than pencil.

 OOK ILLUSTRATIONS

How many people on seeing a pretty book illustration would think of trying to track down and acquire the original? Relatively few, I would imagine, and yet this is an enjoyable and extremely rewarding way in which to start a collection. One only has to look at the work of the great nineteenth- and early-twentieth-century illustrators such as Arthur Rackham, Sir John Tenniel, and Beatrix Potter to realize the potential value of this genre.

Children's book illustrations make an ideal subject for collecting by couples with young children. As anyone who has read aloud to children will know, some illustrations captivate whereas others are ignored; some are just as satisfying to the adult eye as to the child's.

Whatever your taste—or that of your child—this is an area in which it is still possible to acquire original works for relatively little. By dint of a little detective work, starting perhaps with the publisher whose book you admire, you may be able to track down the illustrator who will be only too happy to sell either the book illustrations or other work. I first spotted the work of Christine Thouzeau while reading to one of my children, and I have since commissioned several works from her for my gallery.

ABOVE: Frank Adams, a watercolor and pen-and-ink work for *Alice's Adventures in Wonderland*, 1912. LEFT: William Pene DuBois, a watercolor for *The Night Book*, by Mark Strand, 1985.

Although Helen Craig does not sell her illustrations, many illustrators do. This watercolor and pen-and-ink illustration is from *Angelina Ballerina*, by Katherine Holabird, 1983.

ABOVE LEFT: Johnny
Gruelle, watercolor and
pen-and-ink for *Raggedy
Ann's Lucky Pennies*, 1932.
ABOVE RIGHT: Maud
Humphrey, watercolor,
1895. LEFT: Helen Jacobs,
watercolor and pen-and-ink
for *The Land of Never
Grow Old*, c. 1920. RIGHT:
Kate Greenaway, watercolor
for *Hop o' My Thumb*, folk
tale, c. 1871.

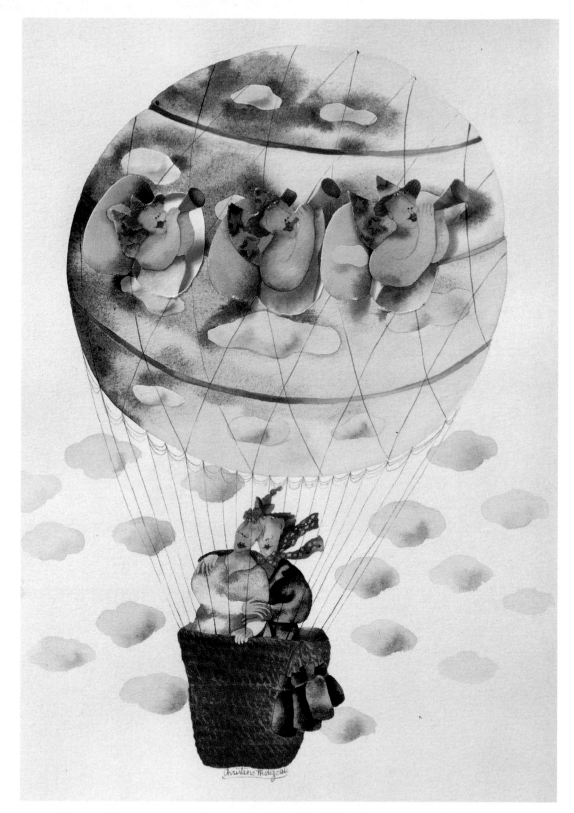

ABOVE: Christine Thouzeau, watercolor. ABOVE RIGHT: Alice Bolam Preston, watercolor for *The Strange Year,* by Eliza Orne White, c. 1920. BELOW RIGHT: Tony Sarg, watercolor and pen-and-ink for *Children Forever,* by John F. MacPherson, 1908.

LIVING ARTISTS

Many of the paintings I have presented are the work of living artists. This is an increasingly interesting area for collecting. Some years ago, when I, like most other picture dealers, had to face the ever-dwindling supply of good old paintings, watercolors, drawings, and prints, I started to look at what was available from living artists. I became aware that as prices of old—and even not-so-old—pictures were becoming prohibitively high, one could still buy the work of very able living artists for relatively little.

To start with, my tastes were very traditional and I was more interested in contemporary artists who were painting in past styles. I had the good fortune to meet José Escofet, the Catalan still-life painter, and marvelous craftsmen such as Dan Dunton and Paul Stagg, both of whom paint in the primitive style. But, recently, my taste has widened and I have become interested in the work of several Spanish artists, including Manuel Blesa and Pedro Darder. Because Spain has been isolated

for so long, their work has a unique quality. I also came across George Sheridan, an artist who has lived in the Mediterranean and whose work, very much an *homage à* Matisse, is full of southern warmth. In France I discovered the childlike naïveté and happiness of the work of Marie Amalia and the marvelous still lifes painted by her mother, Susie Bartolini.

I am also very much interested in contemporary portraiture, which seems to me to be an art revived as people rediscover the uniqueness of a painted portrait over the ubiquitous photograph. Great portraits, as indeed great photographs, never date, and there can be no more relevant form of living artistry to commission and hang in your own home.

I do not pretend to know a great deal about the contemporary American art scene, but from time to time on my travels across the United States, I happen across a gallery showing the work of an artist I find appealing. Many of the vacation towns of America have

OPPOSITE TOP: *Kirby House, Berkshire*, ink pen, by John Warrender.
OPPOSITE BOTTOM: *Monkey on a Basket*, oil on canvas, by Richard Johnson.
LEFT: A family portrait in oil by Howard Morgan.

Three bowls of flowers in
different media. ABOVE:
Pastel by Elsie Eastman.
TOP RIGHT: Watercolor by
Rosemary Clark Stiefel.
RIGHT: Oil on canvas by
Mitch Billis.

Red Tulips, acrylic, by
Connecticut artist
June Owen.

wonderful art galleries: Nantucket and Los Angeles are two examples, while Santa Fe seems to be an art lover's paradise. Illustrated here are a selection of works by some of the artists I have stumbled across in this manner.

All the artists mentioned in this chapter are now quite well known, but when I first discovered them, they were totally unknown. There are always up-and-coming artists whose work is un-dervalued and underappreciated and by dint of judicious looking around at first showings or end-of-year shows at art schools, it is still possible to spot a future star and snap up a bargain at the same time.

Do not, however, forget my original maxim: Only buy what you really like. A picture must be something that gives you pleasure each time you look at it —that is your true investment.

ABOVE: **Gouache-on-paper triptych by George Sheridan.** LEFT: *The Other Texan*, **acrylic, by Lynne Loshbaugh.**

ABOVE: Serigraph of a Navajo Chief Blanket by Jack Silverman. BELOW: Two mixed media pictures by Lynne Loshbaugh. *Talking Snake Series: The Fall from Grace* (LEFT) and *Chapinita* (RIGHT).

Once you have collected, or begun to collect, your pictures, you will want to give some thought to how to display them. How you choose to arrange them has as much impact on your overall scheme as the subjects you've chosen. On the following pages I will discuss pictures for particular rooms and show illustrations of rooms in which existing collections are interestingly and appropriately hung.

Above all, hanging pictures should be fun.

LIVING WITH PICTURES

It is like putting the icing on the cake, once all the horrors of decorating and perhaps building, moving, and unpacking are over. Do not be frightened to experiment—a few nail holes in the wall won't matter—it's the only way to learn. And, happily, the more you play at "musical pictures," the more confidence you will gain and the more you will enjoy the dramatically different effects you can achieve, simply by rearranging your pictures and objects.

LEFT: **Before**—A 19th-century French floral watercolor hangs above the fireplace, flanked by a pair of smaller pictures and two decorative rococo sconces.
RIGHT: **After**—The sconces remain but the arrangement of pictures alters entirely, this time focusing on an unusual 17th-century painting of the Peruvian Cuzco school.

CHANGING A ROOM WITH PICTURES

I am not a wasteful person and I do not like change for change's sake, but I wanted to create a different look in my London house with the minimum amount of disruption and effort. No architects, builders, decorators, or upholsterers. A case of recycling rather than ripping out.

My drawing room was dominated by a series of eight seventeenth-century portraits, all of members of the same Franco-Italian family and all hung, unframed, above a large sofa. To change the feel of the room, I had to start there. I moved a large pine bookcase from the other side of the room, took off its doors, had it painted to look like an eighteenth-century French break-front, and then filled it with books, objects, and, of course, pictures. Displaying pictures among books is a wonderfully effective and different way to create a feature in a room. The eight portraits were dispersed around the room, but in ones, twos, and threes.

I also completely changed the pictures and objects on and over the man-

tel and reorganized some of the furniture. The needlepoint rug is now in my apartment in New York; the green wing chairs are in another room. (My feelings about regrouping pictures apply equally well to my other possessions!) The only major alteration was the substitution of rich raspberry pink curtains in place of my existing pastel ones. The walls, upholstery, and floor covering all remain the same color, and yet, thanks to the pictures, the feeling of the room is dramatically different.

The landing outside the drawing room was arranged in a very traditional manner with a gilt-framed mirror flanked by pictures. Given that this was a relatively small wall and featureless space, I decided to group all my pictures of interiors here, mixing styles, sizes, and frames in an informal clutter. The result has been to make an intimate corner out of a previously underused space. I had the walls throughout the hall and stairs repainted with a soft Fortuny stencil on cream: a highly effective background for pictures.

By contrast, the decoration in my bedroom remains exactly the same, but the look of the room has been com-

OPPOSITE: After—The bookcase in its new guise, filled with pictures, both hung and propped, photographs, framed collections of intaglio seals, glassware, and books.
ABOVE: Before—dominating the room, the group of eight 17th-century family portraits, its rigid symmetry offset by the asymmetrical arrangements of pictures and objects to the right and left.
LEFT: After—A detail of the bookcase.

LEFT: After—A formerly unused area of wall on the landing became home for a close-hung group of pictures of interiors.

RIGHT: After—A detail of my dressing table showing photographs of my children in tortoiseshell frames grouped around a mirror. In front is a collection of 19th-century gold-and-enamel-topped scent and powder bottles.

pletely altered. Over and around my bed—still piled with my favorite antique linen—I hung all my pictures of cherubs, replacing a group of ecclesiastical architectural renderings and a pair of Portuguese painted panels. Some of these angels or *putti* cost just a few pounds, some a lot more, but together they look very special. I have mixed different frames and, here and there, added a piece of carving to create another dimension. And, in a subtle touch that I love because again it allows for interplay between objects and pictures, I have taken down a quintet of prints of gold perfume bottles—designed by Gustave Keller for the Czar—and put out my own collection of real-life gold perfume bottles.

So you see not only how much fun you can have with pictures but also how essential a part they play in giving a very personal·look to the decoration of a house.

LEFT: After—Angels and putti in a variety of media cover the walls of the main bedroom. ABOVE: Before—A pair of Portuguese painted panels hung to either side of the bed. RIGHT: Before—Detail from the bedroom of a pair of prints of perfume bottles designed by Gustave Keller for the Czar. TOP: After—A detail of the bed, which shows an effective grouping of pictures paired with a decorative carving.

ROOMS TO LIVE IN

LEFT: **An enchanting living room in New Jersey displaying a wonderful series of tulip watercolors propped informally on the mantelpiece.**
ABOVE: **Botanical prints and watercolors are massed around the fireplace in this London drawing room.**

The living room, drawing room, sitting room—whatever you like to call it—is the room in which your own taste is probably most clearly expressed. Cozy and comfortable or stark and sophisticated, this is the room in which you relax and, equally important, in which you entertain. It can be a very grand room, it can be quite informal, but it is usually the setting for the best furniture and pictures in the house.

Unlike an entrance hall or stairway, the living room is a place for arriving rather than passing through. Start your picture planning by studying the various viewpoints: the view from the doorway, from the sofa, from the most comfortable armchair. Use objects such as mirrors and wall lights to full advantage, and do not forget the ef-fects that can be created by combining pictures with objects on tabletops, mantels, or bookcases. Subject matter depends entirely on your personal taste. I love a marvelously eclectic variety, but generally avoid the one-picture—one-wall syndrome. Even over a fireplace, a group of small pictures or one large one flanked by groups of small ones looks much more lively.

A profusion of flower
pictures, grouped to
stunning effect against a
fabric wall, is given added
life by the real arrangements
spilling from the sconces and
massed on the chest below.

ABOVE: **The opposite effect —here Marifé Hernandez has made this single dramatic modern painting the focus of the room.**

LEFT: An elegant tabletop still life featuring a painted still life on an easel. ABOVE: A pair of fruit paintings hung from striped ribbon makes a pretty feature between two sets of flowered curtains.

LEFT: Paneled walls offer a
neat framework for hanging
a series of pictures; the
botanical subject matter
used here is nicely echoed
in the cushions.

LEFT: A more somber
masculine group of pictures
surrounds a marble fire-
place with an interesting
alternative to a traditional
wall hanging offered by the
architectural rendering on
the easel.

ABOVE: An unusual
juxtaposition of a Miró
with a late-18th-century
pastel, combined to eye-
catching effect in Marifé
Hernandez's library.

RIGHT: Dark walls and
dark-patterned chintz make
a dramatic setting for
this bold modern painting.

OPPOSITE: A quartet of floral engravings is given added presence with a decorative use of rope in this drawing room designed by Joanna Wood. LEFT and BELOW LEFT: Two striking examples of symmetry and order in rooms designed by Joanna Wood. BELOW RIGHT: A trio of small pictures is anchored by a large Venetian glass mirror, which, in a neat play on space, reflects its twin on the other side of this sophisticated drawing room.

ℳAKING A GRAND ENTRANCE

Entrance halls are often difficult areas when it comes to hanging pictures. Few homes, especially in cities, have grand entrances, and the majority are awkwardly proportioned and often dark and dreary. However, the entrance hall gives the visitor that important first impression of your home, and is well worth time and thought.

Avoid the temptation to fill the walls with the ragtag end of your picture collection—pictures that do not seem to· fit in anywhere else. The entrance hall

is an ideal place to hang small collections—perhaps only three or four items in each—that you may have amassed, and a lovely eclectic mixture of subjects and media makes for an interesting first impression. Mirrors are especially useful here, both as centerpieces for arrangements of pictures and because the reflection can make a cramped space feel more spacious.

Stairways are particularly tricky areas. Pictures on stairs are seen first from a distance—giving an overall

Two elegant examples of pictures grouped around a central mirror. ABOVE: A variety of media and subject matter, each differently framed. RIGHT: By contrast, an identically framed group of engravings by Besler.

ABOVE: Early-19th-century watercolors of Arcs de Triomphe, all by the same artist, make a dramatic feature. ABOVE RIGHT: Massed almost frame-to-frame, flower prints through the ages virtually paper the walls of Barry Ferguson's Oyster Bay home. OPPOSITE: A series of imposing architectural renderings hang in stately progression.

view—and then close up but sideways on—giving a totally different effect. The overall view is, to me, the most important one, as people rarely linger long enough on a stairway to study the pictures closely. It's the effect that counts. There are two alternative ways to create an interesting and pleasing effect. One is to hang a mass of pictures with a common theme: pictures of places you have visited, small inexpensive engravings prettily framed, or even a collection of family photographs. The other possibility, provided you have a large enough wall on your stairway, clearly visible from above and below, is to hang something very large and impressive, such as a portrait. It will achieve maximum impact and give you and everyone else pleasure every time you pass by.

The fireplace in Kelly Hoppen's drawing room, shown in its original guise, LEFT, and with its new look, OPPOSITE, illuminated by candles.

$\mathcal{T}$AKE THREE FIREPLACES

As a lighthearted exercise, I set out one day to prove how easily one can change the mood and feel of a room just by rearranging the pictures and decorative accessories. My experiment revolved around fireplaces in three London drawing rooms: my own, my son Michael's, and my daughter Kelly's.

Kelly Hoppen is an interior designer and her elegant drawing room focuses on one tiny seventeenth-century religious painting in an ornate gold frame. The mantel below displays a gold sunburst clock, a gilded plaster bust, and a collection of red lacquer boxes. We replaced the painting on the wall with a larger, unframed picture of a Victorian Scottish lady in a Paisley shawl and then ransacked our combined homes for candlesticks which we grouped en masse on the mantel. The Paisley shawl in the painting echoed the Paisley fabrics that Kelly had used in the room and brought the whole scheme together in the most pleasing way. The collection of candlesticks not only looked marvelously warm and romantic when lit but showed just how fascinating the interplay of objects and pictures can be.

OPPOSITE: **Michael's fireplace showing the original arrangement of 17th-century Venetian engravings.** ABOVE: **The new grouping of 19th-century classical drawings.**

Michael Hoppen is a photographer and his taste tends toward very graphic black-and-white pictures. Originally, above the severe black marble mantel in his drawing room, he had an arrangement of six seventeenth-century Venetian engravings, five of similar shape and size in identical frames grouped around a larger one. The effect was very striking, very sophisticated, very stark. We swapped these for a collection of nineteenth-century classical drawings, still monochromatic and still in similar black-and-gold frames, but warmer and softer. The objects on the mantel were changed or rearranged to the same effect: a marble bust gave way to a bronze, the glass came off the ivory dome, and a group of neoclassical intaglio seals were added. Again, these changes were minimal, very much in the taste and style of the owner, and yet provide a quite different effect. A setting that had been dramatic and charged became soothing and restful, without losing any of its originality. The new version also shows how a fireplace arrangement can work without one central picture.

My own fireplace in two different guises: ABOVE, the latest, with a mass of small
pictures grouped around an unframed 19th-century Russian portrait; OPPOSITE,
shows the earlier arrangement, focusing on the Peruvian Cuzco Archangel Gabriel.

My own white marble mantel was surmounted by a wonderful seventeenth-century painting of the Peruvian Cuzco school, depicting the Archangel Gabriel. An extraordinary blend of Jesuit Catholicism and Inca artistry, this painting came to me in its ornate gilt frame and was "anchored" by a trio of little portraits and antique mirrors to either side. With the candlesticks, the red Venetian glass hand bells, and the vase of overblown peonies on the mantel itself, the effect was grand and formal without being overwhelming.

By changing very little, I was able to completely alter the mood. "Gabriel" gave way to an unframed portrait of a Russian aristocrat, which, though grander and more sophisticated, makes for a less formal feel. The mantel displays many more pictures, both on easels and propped against the wall, and the arrangement of flowers is simpler. The top two portraits were exchanged for two slightly bigger ones, which, together with the larger, unframed central picture, lend the whole composition more weight. And so, with few alterations, the mood became less formal, and much more intimate.

ROOMS TO DINE IN

A dining room should ideally be a room only seen by flickering candlelight, laid with fine china, crisp linen, and gleaming silverware, and hung with appropriately imposing pictures—somber portraits or moody landscapes or rich still lifes, the choice is endless. However, in reality, most of us have dining rooms that serve more than one purpose, doubling up as libraries, studies, sitting rooms, or kitchens, and so the choice and the grouping of pictures becomes more complicated.

I prefer my dining area to be warm and welcoming, with subdued lighting, and my choice of pictures tends toward the more moody and evocative. I particularly favor what I term "dining-room pictures," namely those all-too-rare nineteenth-century still-life paintings of dining rooms, featuring perhaps objects on a sideboard, or a table setting with the coffee just stirred in the cup and the napkin in disarray.

My own dining room is blue and white, though I often change the pictures (as you will see in the next chapter). Here, I have hung blue-and-white plates, but I have also countered them with a variety of pictures of unrelated hues. Here, again, the choice depends on personal taste and on the sort of atmosphere and effect that you want.

If your dining room is combined with another area, pictures can be a useful way of giving it an identity of its own. By hanging a collection of pictures, on whatever theme, on the walls of the dining area, you immediately define that area as distinct from the rest of the room. Alternatively, the other half of the room can be used to lend atmosphere to the dining area: a kitchen dresser or library bookcase could very effectively hold pictures as well as china or books. In every case, however, diners are a captive audience, and the pictures they see from their position at the table will contribute enormously to their enjoyment of the meal.

An interesting juxtaposition of china, books, and pictures.

LEFT: Two botanical prints propped against the mirror provide an informal counterpoint to the rococo grandeur of this dining room. RIGHT: Interior designer Mimmi O'Connell has used one large picture to maximum advantage in this dramatic candlelit room.

Botanical engravings by Maria Sybilla Merian hung on a trellised wall
create a point of interest in this house in New Jersey, designed by
Fritz Krieger.

ABOVE: A painting of the 17th-century Peruvian Cuzco school,
in its original carved wood frame. BELOW: Four identically
framed hand-colored engravings by Besler, dated 1613,
make a strong feature above this sideboard.

RIGHT: Blue-and-white tulipières by Escofet echo the tones
of the fabric and china in my dining room in London.

𝒲ORKING WITH BLUE & WHITE

The combination of blue and white is a classic one and one of my particular favorites. From early Chinese porcelain to toiles de Jouy to contemporary fabrics and ceramics, it is a combination that has always appealed to people the world over. It has a cleanness and freshness all its own, and yet it also combines well with other color schemes, adding a new dimension to a yellow room, for example, or lightening and enlivening a darker room.

My own dining room is all blue and white, taking its cue from my collection of Worcester and Chinese export plates and echoing in the curtains of Fortuny fabric. I love the combination of the plates on the wall with the still life depicting fruit in a blue-and-white dish. Paintings with blue and white in them are always popular—José Escofet's flowers in blue-and-white pots, for example—and a blue-and-white scheme offers endless possibilities for the interplay of objects, pictures, and decoration.

Blue and white works well in both traditional and contemporary decorative schemes. It will always have truly timeless appeal.

Still life by José Escofet.

LEFT: A very early 18th-century découpage mounted on blue paper, from the set hung in my dining room, RIGHT. A detail of my dining room features a painting of blue-and-white china, which is offset by some real examples.

OPPOSITE: *Trompe l'oeil* Chinese pots on this summerboard by Hugh Robson are matched with some three-dimensional examples to either side. ABOVE: A mass of flower prints and fresh flowers enhance this all blue-and-white bedroom designed by Joanna Wood.

LEFT and ABOVE: Two studies of flowers in blue-and-white pots by Escofet.

Bedrooms

If our homes have become our sanctuary from the ugliness and aggression of society, then nowhere is this more apparent than in the bedroom. Four-poster beds, romantic curtain treatments, and yards of chintzy fabric all express this desire for a retreat evoking the values of an idyllic rural past.

Pictures for bedrooms have consequently become more important, particularly if the view from the bedroom window is less of green and rolling countryside and more of brick and concrete. Traditional English country house bedrooms tended to display perhaps a portrait of Grandma, perhaps a watercolor or two or a faded photograph, and it still is true that lots of unrelated but pretty items come together well in a bedroom setting. Combinations of flower watercolors, botanical prints, small portraits, and rural scenes work particularly well with the country look, but all sorts of small groupings can be used to create these highly personal, intimate retreats.

OPPOSITE: An 18th-century painted panel makes an appropriate backdrop for this handsomely carved and painted French bed. ABOVE: A theorum, a form of stencil painting, in watercolor, dating from around 1800.

Two variations on a theme in the same bedroom, showing how minimal changes can alter the mood. ABOVE: The bed is covered in a blue quilt and three small botanical prints hang above the bedhead. ABOVE RIGHT: The quilt has gone and two large Chinese baskets of flowers in fine gold and gesso frames occupy the wall.

A set of classically framed prints of perfume bottles flanks the window in my London bedroom.

A dramatic setting for a
dramatic picture: This oil of
flowers is hung—and lit—
within the canopy of this
floral chintz four-poster.

ABOVE: Four Besler engravings in original color and handmade frames were chosen to complement the chintz used in this bedroom designed by Van Hattum & Simmons. LEFT: A mirrored panel behind the bed doubles the impact of these drawings, superbly arranged to lend a studious ambiance of this stylish bedroom in a Park Avenue penthouse. RIGHT: A design for the back of a small sofa, executed in watercolor toward the end of the 19th-century, makes a decorative and unusual bed-back in this bedroom.

The 19th-century watercolor *trompe l'oeil* of a jumbled miscellany, LEFT, is an excellent example of this once-popular genre. RIGHT: A cleverly hung wall of pictures of various media and subject matter creates an essentially masculine yet very individual and interesting effect.

COZY MASCULINITY

Whenever a room is decorated as a study or library or any other room intended primarily for masculine occupancy, the pictures tend to fall into one of several well-defined categories: sporting, even for men who have never held a gun or rod in their lives; black-and-white engravings of stately homes; college photographs; or animal or bird paintings. I do not dismiss any of these if they are the occupant's true passion but I do question their automatic use in cases where the occupant actually prefers the ballet or Beethoven to a Scottish grouse moor.

A man's study should mirror his interests through the pictures and objects. These could be photographs or portraits of his family; they could be theatrical posters, designs for the ballet or opera, botanical prints; they could be anything. Recent studies that I have done have ranged pictorially from a collection of Bakst ballet costume designs to drawings of railway stations: they both looked marvelous, reflected the interests of their owners, and were refreshingly unstereotyped.

If the man is not driven by any particular passion, pictures of architectural facades are always good because they have so many associations.

A detail of Bill Blass's entrance hall showing part of his collection of 18th-century and 19th-century architectural drawings.

LEFT: One wall of a New York library shows a very stylish arrangement of pictures grouped around a large architectural watercolor. ABOVE: A quartet of architectural découpage in unusual marquetry frames.

A library in New York designed by Bunny Williams featuring a collection of architectural drawings.

ABOVE and RIGHT: Two
interesting juxtapositions of
pictures and objects play
upon the classic masculine
theme to very unusual effect.

OPPOSITE: One wall of Bill
Blass's bedroom featuring
a superb collection of
drawings, effectively framed
and hung.

THREE WOMEN OF STYLE

LEFT: A classic combination of picture, objects, and console table in the dining room of Bunny Williams's Connecticut home. RIGHT: The veranda is an unlikely but highly effective place for this large, unframed canvas.

The women featured here are dissimilar in many ways, but they are linked by one important characteristic: Each has a highly individual sense of style. They do not follow any "rules," though each is a renowned expert in her field; they don't worry about what is considered to be good taste or bad taste. They work instead according to their own precepts and therefore stand out from the crowd.

BUNNY WILLIAMS

Bunny Williams decided from an early age to focus on interior design, and her sense of style has been influenced by a variety of factors. Born into an old Virginia family, she now has a house in Connecticut, and her schemes reflect this duality, combining the feeling of the North and New England with traditional Southern living. She spent twenty-two years with the design firm Parish-Hadley before setting up her own business and was tremendously influenced by the work of Sister Parish. She has a wide knowledge of art and antiques, fostered by a brief period working in the antiques trade and reflected in her own marvelous private library of reference books. Schooled in the classics, she designs rooms that are very American, with a relaxed informality which belies meticulous planning and an awareness of the importance of architectural design. She has a strong sense of discipline and her schemes adapt as easily to a Fifth Avenue New York apartment as they do to a country house.

LEFT: A view of a long kitchen—very much the heart of the home—focusing on the pair of découpage pictures by Bunny Williams herself that hang over the mantelpiece, detail above. RIGHT: In the library, a fine French 18th-century portrait is hung to great effect in front of the rows of books in the bookcase.

Pictures and objects are arranged with an inimitable sense of style in the library. Note the picture against the bookcase and the small picture propped on the mantelpiece, OPPOSITE. LEFT: An eclectic and highly personal collection of flower pictures is featured in the main bedroom. The chintz corona above the bed makes a pretty frame for a small oval flower picture, while two floral plates on sconces add another dimension above the dressing table.

OPPOSITE: A marvelous mélange of media and style characterizes this collection of flower pictures in Sister Parish's bedroom. LEFT: A watercolor of parrots in an oval frame holds its own against a highly elaborate wallpaper background.

$\mathcal{S}$ISTER PARISH

Doyenne of American interior design, Sister Parish is quite simply a legend in her own lifetime. She turned to decorating in the 1930s and now, sixty years later and in her eighties, is still at the forefront of the interior design world. She was the first to introduce to America what is known as the English country house style, which should really be called the Sister Parish style. She was never formally trained in interior design, but her natural sense of style is inimitable. She creates wonderfully warm and comfortable rooms, rooms that invite you to come in, sit down, move things about; rooms, in fact, that are for living in. Her client list is long and impressive, and her work elicits every superlative in the book from both her colleagues and her rivals. She sets styles, does not follow them, and those who try to follow her never quite achieve the same masterly originality and flair.

LEFT: A corner of the library, featuring two still-life paintings in original frames neatly hung one above the other, creating a point of interest on a narrow wall. ABOVE: A wall of different flowers portrayed in different media in the bedroom, framed by a floral wallpaper border and flowery cushions.

GENEVIEVE WEAVER

Genevieve Weaver is the founder and owner of Guinevere Antiques, one of the best known and most respected antiques dealerships in London. She came to England from her native France in 1954 and nine years later set up shop on the same site—Number 576 King's Road, SW3—that she occupies today. She was among the first to establish an antiques business in what is now one of London's main antiques thoroughfares, and throughout her career, she has demonstrated that instinct—she calls it her "nose"—for the style and fashion of the moment. Her house in Fulham combines her love of objects and pictures with her own confident sense of decoration. "I tend to start with one outstanding piece—an object, a picture, a piece of furniture—and then go on from there," she explains. Her houses (this is the sixth she has occupied since she came to London) are always "on the move," with pictures and objects being added, subtracted, or simply reorganized to create different effects.

TOP: Flanking a Venetian mirror, watercolor designs echo silver objects in the dining room. ABOVE and OPPOSITE: The drawing room features part of Genevieve Weaver's extensive collection of Pierrot paintings and objects, offset by marvelous antique furniture.

LEFT: A collection of paintings of interiors is grouped to great effect over massed ranks of clear-glass decanters, glasses, and jugs. ABOVE: Architecture makes an unusual but highly effective theme for the pictures in the main bedroom, the strong, conventionally masculine renderings offset by soft fabric-covered walls.

DISPLAYING
PICTURES

A frame should not only carry out its functional duty of enabling you to hang your picture on the wall, it should define and enhance the picture and it should provide a "bridge" between that picture and the room in which the picture hangs.

The first task in framing a picture is to assess its character. A primitive oil of a dog or a sheep will lend itself well to framing in simple, rustic wood; a traditional watercolor or fine master drawing will look better in a gran-der gold or gilt frame. If the picture is part of a series, do you want to frame them all identically or differently? The former can look chic and sophisticated, but I, personally, love the effect created by a wall of differently framed items. The second consideration is the room in which the picture is to hang, but do not be too hidebound by your decoration. In the same way that a garden is made up of many colors and many species, so a room benefits from variety.

There is an important distinction to be made between handmade and manufactured frames: the latter are made from mass-produced moldings, cut down and mitered to fit any size of picture; the former are fashioned to fit a specific picture. With a handmade frame, the joinings are concealed. The difference is like comparing a couture garment to a mass-produced one and is reflected, of course, in the price.

A huge array of different frames or frame moldings is daunting to the untrained eye. Make a note of frames that you see in other people's houses, in galleries, in museums, and in magazines, so that when you take your picture to be framed you have an idea in mind of the effect that you are hoping to achieve; best of all, take a sketch or photograph or cutting with you. A good framer will select just three or four "corners" to lay round your picture for you to choose from. Always remember that one is inclined to choose a frame molding that is too narrow: scale up by several sizes and you are more likely to be satisfied.

Finally, remember that there is a good case for occasionally reframing your pictures. First, as we have already established, you can give an old picture a whole new lease on life with a different frame, and second, it enables you to keep a check on the condition of your picture.

RIGHT: A painted wood matt, set within a simulated ivory frame.
BELOW: An elegant threefold surround of handmade marbled paper set into a dark-green paper, then set into a lighter-toned paper.

This handmade frame and blue matt were designed to harmonize with this unusual late-18th-century blue print of the Armada.

MATTING PICTURES

Matting is a difficult subject because it is very much a matter of personal taste. Several years ago, when the vogue for unusual and highly decorative matts was only beginning, I had great fun experimenting with all kinds of different effects. Today, this look is everywhere: every mail-order catalog offers matted prints for sale, and every framer has a huge stock of ready-made matts. With a few notable exceptions, matting tends to look dated, and I much prefer the freshness and newness of close framing.

The exceptions to this rule include traditional watercolors, which from the eighteenth century onward have always been framed with fine French hand-washed matts in dusty colors and using hand-milled gold foil. This combination is timeless and still looks wonderful today. Another exception is when one is framing a group of, say, small sketches or designs, fitting several items into a single frame, when a matt helps give order and definition to the composition.

There is a school of thought which believes that elaborate marbled and painted matts can make even the most unimportant print look impressive. It is worth remembering, however, that these sort of matts tend to become dated. Also, unless they are done superbly well—using hand-marbled paper and hand-milled gold foil—the effect may not be successful.

As a general rule, keep matts simple and classic. Try to let the picture speak for itself and always consider the option of close framing.

LEFT: Five black-and-terra-cotta hand-colored engravings, grouped and set into a black handmade matt, highlighted with hand-painted terra-cotta lines.

BELOW: A collection of jewelry designs matted together for greater effect, each design outlined with hand-milled gold foil paper.

An octagonal mat and frame give greater definition to this charming Victorian watercolor.

A frame cleverly painted to look like old distressed wood, with a decorative edging.

DECORATED FRAMES

This category refers to frames that are an art in themselves, where special effects or techniques—etching, shaping, *faux bamboo*—or decorative details, such as gilded ropes and tassels or armorial crests, have been used. They are unusual and highly decorative and can be particularly effective when framing a series of pictures.

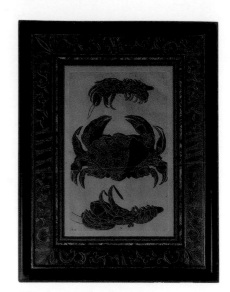

This hand-colored engraving has been close framed with a flat gold Florentine-type surround encased in a simple black frame.

ABOVE: Twigs of bamboo, gilded and dulled down, were twisted to make a nestlike frame for this bird picture. RIGHT: A black frame enlivened by a silver-gilded slip and corner details provides a perfect foil for a black-and-white engraving.

Four examples of different
wooden frames, including
one (ABOVE) in *faux bois*,
or painted wood.

$\mathcal{W}$OOD FRAMES

Wood frames range from ornate veneers and dark polished wood to stained, limed, and natural frames. In the main, they tend to create more of a country look, ideally suited to primitive oils, rustic flower paintings, sporting pictures, and so on. However, a veneered wood frame in, say, mahogany or walnut, with a gilded slip, can look marvelously grand and quite at home in the most urban drawing room: wood is a versatile framing medium.

Four examples of gold and gilt frames. ABOVE: A narrow slip with a gold beveled edge has been inserted to prevent the frame from masking part of the image.

GOLD AND GILT FINISHES

The difference between a gold and a gilt frame is that the former is made with gold leaf, the latter with metal leaf. This category represents the other end of the scale from wood and tends to be much grander, more formal, more urban. Traditional carved or molded gold frames are usually used for oil paintings, although I think they have a much wider application. A watercolor, for example, straight-framed (without a matt) in a beautiful carved frame can look wonderful. As with wood, the range of effects is vast. A highly ornate, molded gold frame will create a quite different look from a simple, narrow gold band. The various media may be mixed: a touch of gold on a wooden frame will transform it into something more grand and formal; the use of wood on a gold frame will add a totally different dimension.

PAINT AND GESSO FINISHES

Paint is one of the cheapest, most cheerful and versatile media for frames. The range of effects from the artist's—or even the amateur's—brush is enormous, from dragging or sponging in pretty pastel shades for a bedroom or bathroom, to glossy black lacquer or exotic tortoiseshell or malachite finishes for drawing or dining room.

Gesso is a material made of gypsum or plaster of Paris, applied in layers and painted onto the frame, which can ultimately be polished to a smooth, seamless sheen. Like paint, it gives full rein to the framer's imagination and the effects are endless. Unlike paint, however, it is one of the most expensive forms of framing.

ABOVE: A hand-painted frame. ABOVE CENTER: A challenge to frame, this painting of a plate from Provence was encased in a gessoed wooden surround that was in turn finished with a painted, ropelike wood frame. BELOW CENTER: A gessoed and painted frame.

TOP: A mat flecked with gold and a three-tiered frame add impact to a simple 18th-century botanical watercolor. ABOVE: A very elaborate form of gesso framing.

HANGING PICTURES

Once your pictures are framed, the next challenge is to group them and hang them in order to show them off to their full advantage. This may involve rehanging some existing pictures or starting completely afresh. Either way, it is daunting.

The floor is a good place to work out your picture placements. By laying the pictures on the floor and moving them around like dominoes, you can get the look you are trying to achieve without lifting a hammer. And when you are ready to hammer, invest in some tiny nails—which leave virtually no marks or buy picture hooks which also leave minimal nail holes—and remember that the odd nail hole does not matter anyway; it will probably be covered by another picture. My walls are like pin-cushions because I like changing my pictures around, but the fun I have and the new look I create every time is well worth any markings.

As is abundantly clear in this book, the minimal look is not one I admire. I have never seen a wall with too many

OPPOSITE ABOVE: Grosgrain bows and rosettes are an easy way to make a wall look full. The pictures appear to be hanging on the ribbon, but they are actually hung on nails. OPPOSITE BELOW: Balance rather than exact symmetry is the key to this grouping of interior pictures. LEFT: Grouping identically framed pictures of the same subject creates a strong visual impact. All inexpensive watercolors, these flower pictures look marvelous together. A bowl of flowers adds to the effect. ABOVE: An awkward landing area was furnished by a fascinating group of interior pictures.

pictures on it, and I find bare walls or walls with one single picture, hanging in a solitary state, rather sterile and sad. Start by looking at your room anew; stand in the doorway and assess what you see. Large pieces of furniture such as a sofa or table against a wall, or a mantel, can be good "bases" for groups of pictures on the wall above. Consider every angle of the room: a previously unused corner might be given a cozy intimacy with a group of three or four little pictures.

Intersperse objects among your pictures to create another dimension. Wall sconces, mirrors, medallions, wood carvings, or plaster plaques all help to anchor a group of pictures. In some cases, you may be able to relate the pictures on the wall to decorative objects on a table or mantel below for added interest; the interplay of objects and pictures offers endless possibilities.

Lastly, don't forget that walls are not the only places to put pictures. I love pictures on easels, or propped on mantels, or hung on cupboard doors. If you have shelves of books, try breaking them up with pictures and decorative objects, or even hang a picture or two in front of the books.

ABOVE: When closed, this concealed doorway is further masked by a trio of pictures. Rather than use the conventional large picture of a porcelain coffeepot, LEFT, we decided to group four small matching watercolors, creating a more interesting look in this awkward dining room corner, OPPOSITE. The effect is heightened by the pictures' two-part frames, the inner piece replacing a more traditional mat. The assortment of actual porcelain objects, ABOVE LEFT, echoes the pictures in color and shape. OVERLEAF: The addition of pictures and objects to the more traditional leather-bound books in this dining room bookcase creates a wonderfully attractive look.

DIRECTORY

◆

SOURCES FOR PICTURES AND FRAMES

LONDON

An excellent place for the visitor to start is to buy the Antiques Trade Gazette, *published weekly on Wednesdays and available either direct from 17 Whitcomb Street, London WC2H 7PL (071-930 4957), or from the newsstand outside Sotheby's, 34 New Bond Street, London W1. The gazette lists details of antiques fairs, country house sales, and auctions in London and throughout the United Kingdom, as well as details of overseas fairs, exhibitions, and sales.*

GALLERIES

The traditional center of the London art scene is the West End and still the area in and around Bond Street is crammed with galleries, both large and small. Bond Street itself tends to the more traditional with well-established galleries such as Agnews,

Colnaghi's, Richard Green, and Malletts. Just around the corner, Cork Street is the mecca for modern art aficionados with lots of small, specialist galleries.

Beyond this starting point, sources of art in London are so extraordinarily diverse and widespread that all I can hope to do here is list a few favorites of my own.

David Ker Fine Art
85 Bourne Street, SW1
071-730 8365
Always has an amusing, very English selection of pictures on show.

Ledbury Road, W11
Full of interesting galleries and shops, including a good stock of old frames.

Gallery Lingard
50 Pall Mall, SW1
071-930 1645
A good source of architectural renderings.

John Mitchell & Son
8 New Bond Street, W1
071-493 7567

The recognized expert on flower painting and his gallery always carries a lovely selection.

Mrs Monro
16 Motcomb Street, SW1
071-235 0326
The doyenne of the English decorating scene and designer of, among many others, a beautiful auricula chintz called Polyanthus; she always has a range of pretty antiques and pictures on show and usually one or two of auriculas.

Raymond O'Shea Gallery
89 Lower Sloane Street, SW1
071-730 0081
Offers traditional English prints and, with Carolyn Warrender Stencil Design next door, presents an inexpensive and effective way of creating a traditional print room.

The Print Room
37 Museum Street, WC1
071-430 0159
Another good source of prints.

Arnold Wiggins & Sons
30–34 Woodfield Place, W9
071-286 9656
specializes in antique frames.

It is also well worth visiting the shops of interior designers, partly because they are sources of attractive antiques and pictures, and partly to see how the pictures are framed and hung:

Nina Campbell
9 Walton Street, SW3
071-225 1011

Joanna Wood
48a Pimlico Road, SW1
071-730 5064
Both have great senses of style.

The following are all specialists in their respective fields and are listed here both for the works of art and antiques that they offer and for their strong individual senses of style.

Anthony Belton
14 Holland Street, W8
071-937 1012
Paintings.

Arthur Davidson
78–79 Jermyn Street, SW1
071-930 4643
A treasure chest, full of the
unexpected.

The Dining Room Shop
84 White Hart Lane, SW13
081-878 1020
All kinds of decorative antiques and
pictures for the dining room.

Dinan & Chichine, W3
by appointment only
081-993 6517
Decorative antique prints.

Graham & Oxley
27 Bury Street, SW1
071-229 1850
Fine botanicals.

Guinevere Antiques
578 Kings Road, SW6
071-736 2917

Linda Helm
117 Richmond Avenue, N1
071-609 2716
19th-century floral watercolors.

Jilly Kelly Antiques
19 Cambridge Street, SW1
071-834 9703

Mallett & Son
40 New Bond Street, W1
071-499 7411

The Map House of London
54 Beauchamp Place, SW3
071-589 4325

Rogers de Rin
76 Royal Hospital Road, SW3
071-352 9007

Keith Skeel
94 Islington High Street, N1
071-226 7012

G. J. Savile
15 Queen Street, W1
071-493 0319
Prints, maps, and caricatures.

Serena Stapleton Antiques
75 Lower Richmond Road, SW15
081-789 4245

Pamela Teignmouth & Sons
108 Kensington Church Street, W8
071-229 1602

AUCTION HOUSES

Bonhams
Montpelier Galleries
Montpelier Street, SW7
071-584 9161
Regular sales of fine art and
antiques.

Chelsea Galleries
65 Lots Road, SW10
071-351 7111
Useful source of lower-priced
furniture and pictures.

Christie's
8 King Street, SW1
071-839 9060
Top of the range fine art and
antiques, jewelry, etc.

Christie's
South Kensington
85 Old Brompton Road, SW7
071-581 7611
Good place for beginners to browse
—lower-priced furniture, rugs,
pictures, etc.

Phillips
101 New Bond Street, W1
071-629 6602
Regular sales of fine art and
antiques.

Sotheby's
34 New Bond Street, W1
071-493 8080
Top-quality fine art and antiques;
regular "fast sales" of lesser quality
items.

All the auction houses are well
worth a visit, even if only to
browse, and information is readily
available on forthcoming sales.

MARKETS AND ARCADES

Alfie's Antique Market
13–25 Church Street, NW8
071-723 6066
Browser's paradise, a rabbit-warren
of stalls, offering a marvelous
mixture of quality and junk. Open
Tuesdays to Saturdays.

Antiquarius
135–141 Kings Road, SW3
071-351 5353
Lots of interesting stalls but
Chelsea prices.

Bermondsey
Bermondsey Street and Long Lance,
SE1
071-407 3635
Lots to see, very good value, but
for early birds only. Friday
mornings, 5:00 a.m.–1:00 p.m.

Camden Lock
Camden Lock Place
Chalk Farm Road, NW1
071-485 7963
Great fun to visit on a Sunday
morning, bargains to be had.

Camden Passage
Islington, N1
071-354 2839
Mixture of antiques shops and
stalls, excellent browsing but very
well known and prices can be high.
Wednesdays and Saturdays.

Chelsea Antique Market
245/253 Kings Road, SW3
071-352 9695
Permanent stalls/shops, interesting
but pricey.

Chenil Galleries
181–183 Kings Road, SW3
071-351 5353
Particularly good for 1920s pieces.

Gray's
Davies Street/Davies Mews, W1
071-629 7034
Huge variety of stalls, West End
prices.

Portobello Road, W11
Maze of little antiques shops and stalls, great atmosphere still but becoming very touristy, get there early. Fridays and Saturdays.

Note: Some of the big London hotels hold regular Sunday markets that are fun to visit. Details from the *Antiques Trade Gazette*.

OUTSIDE LONDON

One of the greatest joys of traveling in the United Kingdom is the chance to discover some marvelous object or picture in one of the numerous little antiques and art shops that seem to have sprouted along the high street of every town and village in the country. The main antiques centers are well known, but well worth a visit, nevertheless: The Lanes in Brighton, Sussex; the Cotswolds; Bath; Suffolk and Norfolk.

The following are some of my favorite places—listed alphabetically rather than geographically:

Adam Gallery
13 John Street, Bath
0225-480406
Specializing in fine 19th- and early-20th-century watercolors and oil paintings.

Julian Armytage
The Old Rectory, Wayford
Near Crewkerne, Somerset
0460-73449
18th-and 19th-century prints.

Cambridge Fine Art
Priesthouse, Little Shelford, Cambridge
0223-842866/843537
Fine British and Continental oil paintings.

Carling & Sinclair
Coconut House, Hall Street
Long Melford, Suffolk
0787-312012
Paintings.

Maureen Morris
Folly Cottage
Littlebury, Saffron Walden, Essex
0799-21338
Samplers.

Paravicini
7 Bridge Street
Hungerford, Berkshire
0488-685172
Oil paintings, watercolors, drawings, prints, and antiques.

Martin Scadgell
Red House Brook
Isle of Wight
0983-740765
Paintings.

Manfred Schotten Antiques
109 High Street
Burford, Oxfordshire
099382-2302
Golfing pictures.

Roger Widdas Fine Paintings
7 Bullivents Close
Bentley Heath, Solihull
Late-19th- and early-20th-century English and European oil paintings and watercolors.

FRAMERS

Autonomy
la Hollywood Road, SW10
071-351 7303

John Campbell
164 Walton Street
London SW3
071-581 1775

Alec Drew
5 Cale Street
Chelsea Green, London SW3
071-352 8716

P. R. Elletson & Co.
Fordbrook Estate
Marlborough Road
Pewsey, Wiltshire
0672-62160

Sebastian D'Orsai
8 Kensington Mall
London W8
071-229 3888

64 Hill Rise
Richmond, Surrey
081-332 1764

39 Theobald's Road
London WC1
071-405 6663

77 Elizabeth Street
London SW1 071-730 8366

F. A. Pollak
3–4 Faulkner's Alley
Cow Cross Street, London EC1
071-490 4413

The following are also useful sources:

Falkiner Fine Papers
76 Southampton Row
London WC1
071-831 1151
Marbled papers.

Fast Frame Franchises
The International Centre
Netherton Park
Stannington, Northumberland
0670-89697

The Frame Factory
20 Cross Street
London N1
071-226 6266

John Lewis Partnership
Oxford Street
London W1
071-629 7711
And branches.

Liberty
210–220 Regent Street
London W1
071-734 1234
Unusual frames and pictures.

The Reject Shop
234 Kings Road
London SW3
071-352 2820

PARIS

When buying goods in France, Italy, or Spain, it is vital first to check whether these goods can be exported without applying to the authorities for permission. Many an unwary buyer has been thwarted at customs, unwittingly trying to leave the country without the correct papers. It is a good idea to check with the trade counsellor of the country in question before you leave home.

Also worth a visit are the Quais, all along the Left Bank of the River Seine, which are lined with small antiques shops and stalls. In the seventh arrondissement, the area within Rue de l'Université, Rue de Bac, the Quai Voltaire, and Rue des Saints-Pères is full of marvelous antiques shops which have grouped together under the collective title of the Carre Rive Gauche. Proute in the Rue de Seine is a particularly good source of prints and drawings, and Madeleine Castaing's legendary antiques shop is at 21 Rue Bonaparte, 75006 (1-4354-9171). For fine antique frames, visit Cadres Vincennes in the Rue de Bac. Finally, even if you do not intend to buy, the Drouot auction rooms at the Hotel Drouot, 9 Rue Drouot, Paris 75009 (1-4246-1711), are well worth a visit. Sales dates are listed in the Gazette de l'Hotel Drouot, published weekly.

MARKETS AND ARCADES

Le Louvre des Antiquaires
2 Place du Palais Royal
Paris 75001
01-4297-2700
A huge covered market in the center of Paris. Tuesdays to Sundays.

Marche Aux Puces
Porte de Clignancourt
Saint-Ouen, Paris
A wonderful source of excellent value antiques, pictures, etc. Open Saturdays, Sundays, and Mondays.

Village Suisse
L'Avenue Motte Picquet
Paris 75015
In the shadow of the Eiffel Tower, offering a varied selection ranging from the antique to the frankly tacky. The occasional bargain.

UNITED STATES

My knowledge of galleries in the United States is obviously limited, so this directory is very eclectic and personal: Santa Fe, for instance, made a huge impression on me. It is said that there are as many (if not more) galleries in Santa Fe than in either London or Paris. It certainly seems that way as you wander through the streets. The difference lies in the relaxed pace of life, in the unique atmosphere, and in the extraordinarily diverse selection of art on show. Navajo Indians sit impassively on the pavements, selling their jewelry and weaving, while the galleries (of which only a few are listed here) offer painting and sculpture, weaving and jewelry, ancient and modern, ethnic and urban—something for everyone.

Of course, I am familiar with New York because I make frequent trips to my gallery there. I have also found Nantucket to be a nice place to wander as well. Alas, my knowledge of Los Angeles and San Francisco is sadly lacking, other than to say that both cities are great sources for pictures, particularly La Cienega Street and Melrose Place in Los Angeles. In any case, I want to pass along this small, idiosyncratic, personal sampling.

ARKANSAS

Mr. and Mrs. Max Harris
Bolton's
5600 Kavanaugh Boulevard
Little Rock, AR 72207
501-666-8626

CALIFORNIA

Janis Aldridge
8452 Melrose Place
Los Angeles, CA 90069
213-658-8456

Ruth Carlson Gallery
Highway One & Main Street
P.O. Box 112
Mendocino, CA 95460
707-937-5154

Every Picture Tells a Story
836 N. La Brea Avenue
Los Angeles, CA 90038
Original art from children's books.

CONNECTICUT

Avis & Rockwell Gardiner
60 Mill Road
Stamford, CT 06903
203-322-1129
A treasure trove of the unexpected.

Guthman Americana
PO Box 392
Westport, CT 06881
203-259-9763

Pat Guthman Antiques
342 Pequot Avenue
Southport, CT 06490
203-259-5743
Kitchen pictures.

Marguerite Riordan
8 Pearl Street
Stonington, CT 06378
203-535-2511
American primitive art.

Stately Antiques
1030 East Putnam Avenue
Riverside, CT 06878
203-637-8585

Peter Tillow Fine Art
Prospect Street
Litchfield, CT 06759
203-567-5706
Fine pictures.

Winsor Antiques
43 Ruane Street
Fairfield, CT 06430
203-255-0056

INDIANA

Red Geranium Enterprises
508 North Street
New Harmony, IN 47631
713-871-8320

MASSACHUSETTS

Janis Aldridge
7 Centre Street
Nantucket, MA 02554
508-228-6673

Don Arbanel Antiques
East Main Street
Ashley Falls, MA 01222
413-229-3330
Eclectic objects.

The Main Street Gallery
50 Main Street
P.O. Box 1450
Nantucket, MA 02554
508-228-4027
I love to wander around Nantucket.
This is one of the nicest galleries
for browsing.

The Sailor's Valentine
40 Centre Street
Nantucket, MA 02554
508-228-2011

MISSOURI

The Chocolate Lady
22 Dromara Road
St. Louis, MO 63124
314-725-2717

NEW HAMPSHIRE

Knotty Pine Antique Market
Route 10
West Swanzey, NH 03469
603-352-5252

NEW JERSEY

Dan Dorsbach
R. H. Macy & Co
30–703 Newport Parkway
Jersey City, NJ 07310
201-560-4666

NEW MEXICO

SANTA FE

Channing–Dale–Throckmorton
53 Old Santa Fe Trail
Santa Fe, NM 87501
505-984-2133

Economos Works of Art
225 Canyon Road and
500 Canyon Road
Santa Fe, NM 87501
505-982-6347

Fenn Galleries
1075 Paseo de Peralta
Santa Fe, NM 87501
505-982-4631

Katie Gingrass Gallery
505-982-5501

Linda McAdoo Galleries Ltd.
503 Canyon Road
Santa Fe, NM 87501
505-983-7182

Morning Star Gallery
513 Canyon Road
Santa Fe, NM 87501
505-982-8187

Gerald Peters Gallery
439 Camino Del Monte Sol
P.O. Box 908
Santa Fe, NM 87504
505-988-8961

David Ross Studio & Gallery
132 West Palace Avenue
Santa Fe, NM 87501
505-988-4017

Santa Fe Print Gallery
Plaza Mercado Upper Level
112 W. San Francisco
Santa Fe, NM 87501
505-984-3211

Sena Galleries East
125 East Palace Avenue
Santa Fe, NM 87501
505-982-8181

Laurel Seth Gallery
1121 Paseo de Peralta
Santa Fe, NM 87501
505-988-7349

William R. Talbot
129 West San Francisco Street
P.O. Box 2757
Santa Fe, NM 87504
505-982-1559

Zaplin-Lampert Gallery
651 Canyon Road
Santa Fe, NM 87501
505-982-6100

Barbara Zusman Art & Antiques
233 Canyon Road
Santa Fe, NM 87501

Taos

Taos Arts Celebrations
120-J Bent Street
Taos, NM 87571
505-758-0516

Weaving South West
216 Paseo del Pueblo Norte
Taos, NM 87571
505-758-0433

New York

America Hurrah Antiques
766 Madison Avenue
NY, NY 10021
212-535-1930
Superb quilts to hang.

W. Graham Arader III
23 East 74th Street
NY, NY 10021
212-628-3668
Americana, fine prints.

Coe Kerr Gallery
49 East 82nd Street
NY, NY 10028
212-628-1340
Fine 20th-century paintings.

The Corner Shop
R. H. Macy & Co.
151 West 34th Street
NY, NY 10001
212-560-4144

R. Gregory Books
222 East 71st Street
NY, NY 10021
212-288-2119

Muriel Karasik
1094 Madison Avenue
NY, NY 10028
212-535-7851
Deco and unusual objects.

Kendra Krienke
230 Central Park West
NY, NY 10024
212-580-6516
Children's book illustrations.

Charlotte Moss
131 East 70th Street
NY, NY 10021
212-772-3320
Botanicals.

Florian Papp
962 Madison Avenue
NY, NY 10021
212-288-6770

The Old Print Shop
150 Lexington Avenue
NY, NY 10016
212-683-3950

Shepherd Gallery
21 East 84th Street
NY, NY 10028
212-861-4050
Architectural prints.

Stubbs Books & Prints
28 East 18th Street
NY, NY 10003
212-772-3120

Ursus Books & Prints
981 Madison Avenue
NY, NY 10021
212-772-8787
Fine prints.

Weyhe Gallery
794 Lexington Avenue
NY, NY 10021
212-838-5478
Good for reference books.

Thomas K. Woodward
835 Madison Avenue
NY, NY 10021
212-988-2906
Quilts for hanging.

Bedford Green Antiques
Village Green, Box 517
Bedford, NY 10506
914-234-9273
Prints.

Florilegium Botanical Art
Snedans Landing
Palisades, NY 10964
914-359-2926
Botanicals.

Raymond B. Knight
121 Birch Hill Road
Locust Valley, NY 11560
516-671-7046

The Millbrook Antiques Center
Franklin Avenue
Milbrook, NY 12545
914-677-9311

Framers

APF
136 East 70th Street
NY, NY 10021
212-988-1090
Excellent work.

Julius Lowy Frame & Restoring Co.
28 West End Avenue
NY, NY 10023
212-586-2050
Elaborate, high-quality work.

J. Pocker
135 E. 63rd Street
NY, NY 10021
212-838-5488

Pennsylvania

Blackmon Galleries
113 West Market Street
Marietta, PA 17547
717-426-2370
Quilts.

Ursula Hobson Framing
1602 Pine Street
Philadelphia, PA 19146
215-546-7889

The Philadelphia Print Shop
8441 Germantown Avenue
Philadelphia, PA 19118
215-242-4750

Washington, D.C.

Janis Aldridge, Inc.
2900 M Street NW
Washington, DC 20007
202-338-7710

Fleming & Meers
Hamilton Court
1228 31 Street NW
Washington, DC 20007
202-343-7777

GLOSSARY

◆

AQUATINT

A variety of etching and essentially a tone process that can be used to imitate the appearance of watercolor. The main element in the process, invented in France in the 1760s, is the partial protection of the surface of the plate with a porous "ground" through which the acid can penetrate. The plate is covered with a ground of powdered resin, which is attached to the plate by heating. In etching, the acid bites tiny rings around each resin grain; when printed, the rings hold sufficient ink to give the effect of a wash.

ARTIST'S PROOF

In twentieth-century printmaking, an artist's proof is an impression signed by the artist and annotated "AP" (or something similar), which is extra to the ordinary numbered edition.

ASCRIBED

A term used when a drawing has been credited to an artist by tradition, often on the strength of an inscription on the drawing or on its mount (mat); it suggests some doubt, however, in the mind of the cataloguer.

ATTRIBUTED

A drawing is "attributed" to an artist on the grounds of style or some good external evidence; however, some doubt remains about its authorship.

BAXTER PRINT

A printing technique patented by George Baxter in 1835, which involved overprinting an intaglio key-plate with numerous wood or metal blocks inked in oil colors.

BODY COLOR

Any type of opaque water-soluble pigment. When first employed in the late fifteenth century, it was composed of lead white. In 1834 Winsor and Newton introduced Chinese white (zinc oxide), which was later substituted for lead white.

CHALK

NATURAL CHALK

Natural chalks are found in various colors and are obtained from earths. For drawing, lumps of these materials were cut to size, inserted into metal holders, and the ends shaved to points.

RED CHALK

Known by the sixteenth century, when numerous Renaissance artists —notably Leonardo da Vinci, Michelangelo, and Correggio— drew in this medium. "Sanguine" is another term for red chalk often found in older reference books.

BLACK CHALK

Similar in origin and initial importance to red chalk. By the late eighteenth and early nineteenth centuries, black chalk had lost much of its popularity due to its variable quality and began to be replaced by black crayons.

FABRICATED CHALKS (PASTELS)

Dry drawing media made from powdered pigments combined with non-greasy binders and used in stick form. The colors can be mixed by smudging—using the fingers or a coil of leather, felt, or paper (a "stump")—or by optical mixing, a method by which the eye "mixes" colors placed side by side. This latter method was especially favored by Degas.

CHARCOAL

Drawing medium made by reducing wood to carbon in heated chambers from which oxygen is excluded in order to prevent combustion from taking place. Charcoal is used frequently as a preparatory medium in drawings intended to be completed in other media. Drawings done entirely in charcoal are usually protected from smudging by the use of a fixative sprayed onto the drawing.

COLLAGE

Term applied to any work composed of pieces of paper or other materials (painted, drawn, or printed on beforehand) stuck onto a supporting surface.

COLLECTOR'S MARKS

Small marks, usually an initial or initials but sometimes a device, stamped or applied by other means, at the corner or in an unobtrusive area on prints or drawings to indicate ownership. Originally, such marks were frequently applied posthumously by executors. Though collector's marks do not denote authenticity, a work with a provenance from one or more important collections is likely to be of high quality.

COLOR PRINTING

There is a clear distinction between "color prints" and "colored prints." A color print is one printed in inks of different colors; a colored print is printed in ink of one color and has had extra coloring added by hand.

CRAYON

Derived from the French *craie*, meaning chalk. Modern crayons are sold in the form of sticks made up of colors combined either with oily, waxy, or greasy binding media, or with combinations of water-soluble and fatty binders.

DRYPOINT

A member of the class of intaglio prints. The line is scratched directly into the plate with a metal point, which is usually, but not invariably, pulled across the surface (and not pushed as in engraving). The displaced metal thrown up on either side of the line is called the "burr." When printed, the burr gives the line a rich, velvety texture, but the line is fragile and wears down quickly with each impression taken.

EDITION

The practice of limiting the number of impressions of a print in order to create an artificial rarity for the collector dates only from the last quarter of the nineteenth century. Today, it is common practice for an artist to sign and number all impressions of a print. Standard numbering uses a form of fraction: 3/20, for example, indicates that the impression was the third in an edition of twenty impressions. In the early days of printmaking, editions were not limited but were printed to meet demand until the plate wore out.

ENGRAVING

A term sometimes used to denote all intaglio prints but correctly applied only to those made with a small, sharp-pointed metal rod called a "graver" or "burin." The graver is pushed across the plate with the palm of the hand, forcing the metal into slivers ahead of the V-shaped line. These metal pieces are then removed with a sharp, bladed instrument known as a "scraper."

ETCHING

A type of intaglio printmaking in which the lines in a metal plate are bitten ("etched" means "eaten") by acid. The polished surface of the plate is first covered with a thin layer of ground, composed of waxes, gums, and resins. The etcher draws through the ground with an "etching needle," which exposes the metal. The plate is then immersed in a bath of acid, which bites into the plate through the exposed lines, leaving the desired image.

GLASS PAINTING OR STAINING

The color in a stained glass window is not painted on the glass surface but incorporated in it during manufacture. Designs for stained/painted glass are still found quite frequently today.

REVERSE GLASS PAINTING

A technique in which paint is applied directly to the reverse of sheets of glass for viewing from the other side. This method appears in the late eighteenth and early nineteenth centuries in southern India, having been introduced by Chinese artisans from South China, Shanghai, and Hong Kong. The same technique was popular in Eastern Europe (notably Czechoslovakia and Poland) in the nineteenth century, particularly for religious subjects. Glass paintings of this type are still produced today in western India.

GLASS PRINT

Printing method used from the end of the seventeenth century to the beginning of the nineteenth, in which mezzotints (generally of mythological or genre subjects) were glued face down onto glass and then abraded from behind in order to remove all of the paper.

The film of ink left behind was then hand-colored and the glass framed.

GOUACHE

A term first used in France in the eighteenth century to describe a method of painting with colors rendered opaque by mixing them with chalks or whites in a gum medium. Its meaning was later extended to apply to a drawing executed in this medium. Today, *gouache* is also used loosely to describe any drawing done completely in body color.

GUM ARABIC

The natural secretion of the acacia tree, which is used in the manufacture of watercolors. Employed chiefly because it assists in the adherence of the pigment to the paper, it also maintains a stable dispersal of pigment particles in water until the film of wash has dried and the colors are gummed in place. This substance is an important factor in determining the appearance of a finished watercolor.

HEIGHTENING

The practice of adding highlights to a drawing or watercolor in either white body color or white chalk. A similar effect can be obtained by scraping through the paint to reveal the white of the paper beneath.

IMPRESSION

The term applied to any print produced from a block, plate, or stone. The word *copy*—as in a copy of a book—should not be used in place of *impression*, since it may imply the additional meaning of *facsimile*.

INK

DRAWING INKS

One of the most widely used, iron-gall ink, was derived from the oak apples of oak trees and was made primarily for writing. Time turns this ink brown, hence the characteristic appearance of many "Old Master" drawings. *Sepia*, a brownish ink obtained from the ink-bag of the cuttlefish, was not in popular use before the end of the eighteenth century.

PRINTING INK

An oil-based fluid completely different from the water-based liquid used for writing, printing ink is made by grinding lampblack very fine and mixing it with oil. It was apparently invented, or at least developed, by Gutenberg.

INSCRIPTION

Any handwriting on a drawing or a print that is not a signature. If an artist's *name* is said to be inscribed, the inference is that it has been added by someone else. An inscription can also be a note by the artist or by a later owner or dealer; it may even have been on the sheet of paper before the artist used it.

INTAGLIO PRINTING
The method used for printing from metal plates which are worked as drypoints, etchings, mezzotints, stipple engravings, and aquatints. The paper receives the ink from the incised lines and not from the plate surface.

LETTERING
A term used to refer to letters engraved on a print. Information about the artist (designer) and engraver is usually given below the bottom left-hand and right-hand corners respectively. The most commonly found terms are listed below. They are mainly Latin in origin.

composuit "Designed," "designer"

cum privilegio Implying the exclusive right to publish, corresponding to modern copyright, granted by some political or ecclesiastical authority.

delineavit (delin), delineator "Drew," "draughtsman"

excudit (excud., ex) "Published"

fecit (Fec., f) "Etched" or "engraved"

invenit (inv.), inventor "Designed," "designer"

lith "Drew" or "printed in stone." This is ambiguous; it can be used by both the lithographic draftsman and the lithographic printer.

pinxit (pinx.), pictor "Painted," "painter"

Published according to Act of Parliament This established copyright in accordance with an act of the British Parliament. The first artistic copyright act was passed in 1735, chiefly due to the efforts of Hogarth.

sculpsit (sculp., sc.), sculptor "engraved," "engraver."

LITHOGRAPHY
Printing technique based on the fact that grease and water repel each other. The image is drawn onto a suitable surface in a greasy medium and printed in the following way: The surface is first dampened with water, which settles only on the undrawn areas (since it is repelled by the greasy drawing medium). It is then rolled up with greasy printing ink, which adheres only to the drawn marks, the water repelling it from the rest of the surface. Finally, the ink is transferred to a sheet of paper by running the paper and the printing surface together through a press.

MEASUREMENTS
Prints and drawings are usually measured in centimeters or millimeters, height preceding width.

MEZZOTINT
This type of intaglio print is essentially a tone process, by which the artist can achieve a range of tone from black, through gray, to white. The surface of a metal plate is roughened all over using a tool with a curved, serrated edge known as a "rocker." If printed at this point, the surface would produce a deep velvety black overall. The artist scrapes down this surface (the "burr") to the lightness of tone that he requires.

MINIATURE
A portrait painted on a small scale with a minute finish, usually on ivory or vellum, but sometimes on card.

MODELLO
A finished study, on a reduced scale, made in preparation for a larger work. Some contracts stated that a modello had to be made, often with a proviso that there be no subsequent changes in the final work.

MONOGRAM
A character usually composed of the initial letters of a name, often interwoven. Monograms are frequently found in place of signatures on prints or drawings.

OFFSET LITHOGRAPHY
Just as in lithography (see entry), the drawing is prepared directly on the stone or (as is more common today) on a metal plate. In offset, however, the inked image is then printed onto a cylinder covered with a rubber blanket from which it is transferred to the paper. With this method, the image when printed appears in the same direction as it was drawn.

OLEOGRAPH
A nineteenth-century process in which an ordinary color lithograph was varnished and/or impressed with a canvas grain in order to make it look like an oil painting.

PAPER
The most common support for drawings, watercolors, and prints. Until the nineteenth century, paper was made from linen or cotton rags, which were beaten with water to form a pulp. A tray of crossed wires (the "mold") was immersed into the mixture, allowing a thin layer of pulp to settle on the top. When turned out and pressed between blankets and dried, the resulting sheet had the quality of blotting paper. Size, a semiviscous liquid made from gelatin, needed to be applied to the surface to make it suitable for drawing or writing on. Most modern paper is made from wood pulp and is of much poorer quality than old handmade paper, though some paper is still made by hand today. "Laid" paper shows the pattern of the "chain lines" of the

wires in the papermaker's tray. "Wove" paper dates from about 1755 and was made from a tray with a tightly woven mesh which left no visible marks.

PARCHMENT

A support for writing (and less often for drawing on) in the Middle Ages and occasionally later, made from the skins of animals, typically sheep or goats. Vellum was a finer quality parchment made from specially selected young skins.

POCHOIR

The French word for a stencil. Pochoir prints were usually hand-colored through a series of carefully cut stencils. This process saw its heyday in Paris during the first thirty years of this century.

PASSEPARTOUT

An ornamental sheet of cardboard with the center cut out, which serves as a mount for a photograph or drawing when framed. A passepartout frame is one ready-made with such a mount. The name has also come to denote a type of framing in which the picture is fastened in place between glass and backboard by the employment of adhesive tape, usually black in color.

SCREEN PRINTING

A type of stencil printing in which a gauze screen fixed tautly on a rectangular wooden frame is laid directly on top of a sheet of paper. Printing ink is spread over the upper side of the mesh and forced through it with a rubber blade (a squeegee) so that it transfers to the paper on the other side.

STIPPLE ENGRAVING

An intaglio tone process where the tone is produced by a profusion of small dots, sometimes engraved but usually etched.

TEMPERA (DISTEMPER)

A type of painting in which dry colors are made usable by mixing them with a glutinous substance soluble in water. The term is also applied to the pigments and to the ground. The standard tempera vehicle is a natural emulsion of egg yolk thinned with water. The egg yolk helps the color to adhere to the support.

VIGNETTE

A small ornamental engraving or design used mainly in book illustration. Its essential feature is that it has no defined border, its edges instead shading off into the surrounding paper.

WASH

In referring to watercolor, the term indicates a broad covering of color by a continuous movement of the brush. In ink drawings, the word often means the use of a dilute ink. Pen drawings are also frequently washed with a different color, such as pen and brown ink with gray wash.

WATERCOLOR

A pigment for which water rather than oil is used as a medium, with gum arabic added as a binder; also commonly used to refer to works done in this medium.

WATERMARKS

Devices used by paper manufacturers. Made of wire and sewn onto the mold (see *paper*), they leave an impression on the paper by making it thinner and also more translucent. Watermarks can help to determine the date and area of origin of the paper, but they cannot always assist in the dating or authentication of the image on the paper. Forgers are generally careful to obtain paper of the correct age to receive their attentions.

WOOD ENGRAVING

A type of woodcut which developed in the eighteenth century. A hard wood (usually boxwood) is used and is cut across the grain. The tool used is not unlike the graver (burin) used in engraving; its handle is held against the palm with the blade pushed before the hand, making a clean cut into the wood. Wood engravings are printed in relief, as are woodcuts, and not in intaglio.

Additional terms and more detailed information regarding terms mentioned here can be found in my book *Looking at Prints, Drawings and Watercolours*, British Museum Publications, 1988.

PAUL GOLDMAN
Curator, Department of
Prints and Drawings
The British Museum

BIBLIOGRAPHY

◆

Armstrong, Tom and Lipman, Jean. *American Folk Painters of Three Centuries.* New York: Hudson Hills Press, Whitney Museum, 1980.

Benall, Julia S. *A History of Flower Arrangement.* London: Thames and Hudson, 1978.

Blunt, Wilfred. *The Art of Botanical Illustration.* London: Collins, 1950.

Chancellor, John. *Audubon.* London: Weidenfeld and Nicolson, 1978.

Clayton-Payne, Victoria. *Victorian Flower Gardens.* London: B. T. Batsford, 1988.

Coates, Alice M. *The Book of Flowers: Four Centuries of Flower Illustration.* London: Chancellor Press, 1984.

Dance, S. Peter. *The Art of Natural History: Animal Illustrators and Their Work.* Woodstock, NY: The Overlook Press, 1978.

Dickson, Elizabeth. *The Englishwoman's Bedroom.* London: The Hogarth Press, 1985.

Drexler, Arthur. *The Architecture of the Ecole de Beaux Arts.* London: Thames and Hudson, 1984.

Dunthorne, Gordon. *Flower and Fruit Prints of the Eighteenth and Early Nineteenth Century.* Washington: author published, 1938.

Earp, T. W. *Flower and Still Life Painting.* London: The Studio, 1928.

Elliot, Brent. *Victorian Gardens.* London: B. T. Batsford, 1986.

Ercoli, Giuliano. *Art Deco Prints.* Oxford: Phaidon, Christie's, 1989.

Fournier, Katou and Lehman, Jacques. *Chats Naifs.* Paris: Galerie Naifs et Primitifs, 1984.

Hardouin-Fugier, Elisabeth and Etienne Grafe. *French Flower Painters of the Nineteenth Century.* London: Philip Wilson, 1989.

Hobhouse, Penelope and Wood, Christopher. *Painted Gardens, English Watercolours 1850–1914.* London: Pavilion, 1988.

Journal of Garden History, Vol. 8, Nos. 2–3, April–Sept. 1988. "The Anglo-Dutch Garden in the Age of William and Mary." London: Taylor & Francis, 1988.

Lysaght, A. M. *The Book of Birds: Five Centuries of Bird Illustrations.* London: Chancellor, 1975.

Middleton, Robin. *The Beaux Art and Nineteenth-Century French Architecture.* London: Thames and Hudson, 1984.

Roma Antiqua Envois des Architectes Français 1788–1924. Paris: Academie de France à Rome, Ecole Français de Rome and Ecole Nationale Superieure des Beaux-Arts, 1985–1986.

Schmidt, Hanspeter. *Menu Designs.* New York: Rizzoli, 1981.

Simon, Robert and Alastair Smart. *John Player Art of Cricket.* London: Secker & Warburg, 1983.

Thornton, Peter. *Authentic Decor, The Domestic Interior 1820–1920.* London: Weidenfeld and Nicolson, 1984.

Vienna in the Age of Schubert (The Biedermeier Interior 1815–1848). London: Elron Press Ltd., 1979.

◆

For me to list all the people—without whose goodwill, good humor, and hard work this book would never have been written—would be impossible. I would have to list all my clients and friends who allowed us access to their homes for photography and who treated us not as intruders but as honored guests.

I would have had to list all the photographers who labored long hours way beyond the call of duty and whose work has made this book what it is.

I would have to thank everyone in my Galleries in London and New York for all the extra hours they cheerfully put in when normal working hours were over to see that all the minutiae of the book were attended to.

I would have to thank all the many people at Clarkson Potter who nurtured me through the pregnancy and labor of producing one's first book. I assume, like childbirth, one forgets and does another.

I would have to thank all my many friends at *House and Garden*, London; *House and Garden*, New York; *House Beautiful*, New York; *Interiors*, London; for their help, advice, assistance, and also photographic material—this was help indeed.

The list of names would be endless and I could never express what I feel; I could never have done this without the help of so many people.

I do feel, however, that I must mention Carol Southern, who has from the very start had faith in me and my concept, and without her confidence and encouragement I might have started this book, but I would surely never have finished it. Her support

and guidance have been something I will always treasure. Together, she and Catherine Haig, my London cohort, nursed me through and brought the book to its conclusion.

All this support has been so generously given and my thanks are from the bottom of my heart.

Major photography by Michael Hoppen, Fritz von der Schulenburg, and Philip de Bay appears on the pages of this book as follows:

HOPPEN, Michael: i, vii bottom left, x top left, xiii top left, xiv, 1, 5 left, 15–18, 19 right, 20 top and bottom right, 22–25, 26 top right and bottom right, 27 top right and bottom right, 28 top and bottom left and right, 29 top right, 30, 31, 34 top and bottom left, 35 bottom left and right, center top and bottom, 37, 39 bottom left, 41 top, 44–55, 56 bottom, 58–59, 60, 61 bottom, 63 top left, 64 top, 66 top right, 69 top and bottom left and top right, 75, 76 top right, 77 left and bottom right, 78, 79 top, 80–85, 88, 91 top and bottom right, 100 top, 102–103, 114, 124–129, 130, 136 top and bottom right, 139, 141, 146, 147, 166–167, 168–173, 174 top right.

VON DER SCHULENBURG, Fritz: ii–iii, vii bottom right, viii, xi, 29 left, 33, 66 bottom right, 67, 68, 90, 111 right, 112, 115, 116 right, bottom left, 117, 119 bottom right, 120–123, 131, 132, 134, 135, 136 left, 137, 138, 140, 142 top left and right, 143, 144, 148, 149, 150, 151–165, 175 top right, 177 right, 178.

DE BAY, Philip: vi, vii top center, ix, x bottom left, right, xiii bottom left and right 3, 4, 5 top and bottom right, 6, 7, 8, 10–13, 14, 19 top and bottom left, 20 bottom left, 26 left, 28 top and bottom center, 29 bottom right, 32, 34 right, 40 bottom, 41 bottom, 42 left, 56 top, 61 top, 62, 63 bottom left and right, top right, 64 bottom, 69 bottom right, 74, 76 top left and bottom, 77 top right, 79 bottom, 95 left, 96 bottom left, 145, 171, 175 left.

ASHWORTH, Gavin: 86, 89, 91; BILLIS, Mitch: 98 bottom right; BOGUE, Gary: 39 top left, 98 top right; BROWN, David: 57, 65, 66 left; BROWN, Simon: 118, 119; DAVIES, Richard: xiii top right, 104 and 107 top, bottom left, courtesy *House & Garden* New York, 142 bottom; EASTMAN, Elsie: 98 left; HENDERSON, Gavin: xiii top left, 2, 9, 41 top, 42 top and bottom right, 43; HUDSON, Nigel: 176, 177 top and bottom left, all courtesy *House Beautiful* London; KRIENKE, Kendra: 92 top, 94, 95 top and bottom right; MARR, Fraser: 96 top left; MONTGOMERY, David: iv, v, 21, 27 left, 174 bottom left; MORSE, Dan: 101 top; MORTIMER, James: 113, 116 top; OWEN, June: 99; SIMMONS, John R.: 97; Speltdoorn et Fils: 70–73; VON EINSIEDEL, Andreas: xii, 87, 105, 106, 107 bottom, 108, 109, 110, 111 top left, all courtesy Condé Nast Publications London, 133; WICKSTROM, Richard: 100 bottom, 101 bottom left and right; WOOD, Christopher: 36, 38, 39 right, 40 top.

Reproduced by kind permisssion of: Christopher Wood Gallery: 36–37, 40; Rafael Valls: 57, 65, 66; *World of Interiors*: 35 top left and right.